1969

HAVE A GOOD TRIP *A sign posted at the Woodstock festival in upstate New York*

TIME

Managing Editor Richard Stengel
Art Director Arthur Hochstein

1969

Woodstock, the Moon and Manson: The Turbulent End of the '60s

Editor Kelly Knauer
Designer Ellen Fanning
Picture Editor Patricia Cadley
Research/writing Matthew McCann Fenton; Matthew P. Wagner
Copy Editor Bruce Christopher Carr

TIME INC. HOME ENTERTAINMENT

Publisher Richard Fraiman
General Manager Steven Sandonato
Executive Director, Marketing Services Carol Pittard
Director, Retail & Special Sales Tom Mifsud
Director, New Product Development Peter Harper
Director of Trade Marketing Sydney Webber
Assistant Director, Bookazine Marketing Laura Adam
Assistant Publishing Director, Brand Marketing Joy Butts
Associate Counsel Helen Wan
Book Production Manager Suzanne Janso
Design & Prepress Manager Anne-Michelle Gallero
Associate Brand Manager Michela Wilde
Assistant Prepress Manager Alex Voznesenskiy

Special thanks to:
Joseph Agnoli, Glenn Buonocore, Susan Chodakiewicz, Neal Clayton, Patrick Dugan, Lauren Hall,
Jennifer Jacobs, Brynn Joyce, Robert Marasco, Amy Migliaccio, Brooke Reger, Ilene Schreider, Adriana Tierno

ISBN 10: 1-60320-065-7
ISBN 13: 978-1-60320-065-3
Library of Congress Number: 2009900530

We welcome your comments and suggestions about Time Books. Please write to us at:
Time Books, Attention: Book Editors, P.O. Box 11016, Des Moines, IA 50336-1016

To order any of our hardcover Collector's Edition books, please call us at 1-800-327-6388 (Monday through Friday,
7:00 a.m.— 8:00 p.m., or Saturday, 7:00 a.m.— 6:00 p.m., Central Time).

To enjoy Time's complete original coverage of the year 1969, visit: **Time.com**

KEN REGAN—CAMERA 5

GREAT EXPECTATIONS *Some folks hitched a lift al fresco on the last leg of the trip to the Woodstock festival in upstate New York*

1969

WARRIOR'S REST *The body of World War II hero Dwight D. Eisenhower*

lies in state in the U.S. Capitol Rotunda, as Americans mourned the two-term President, who died on March 28, 1969

First Impressions

THE PATTERN AT RIGHT WAS STAMPED ON THE surface of the moon by U.S. astronaut Edwin (Buzz) Aldrin on July 20, 1969. And because the moon has no atmosphere and thus no winds, it is very likely that the footprint remains intact, unless it has been disturbed by one of the countless meteorites that collide with the moon each year.

Near the footprint is the bottom half of the landing module that brought Aldrin and Neil Armstrong to the moon's surface, left behind when they returned to Earth. A plaque on its base extends the greetings of President Richard M. Nixon and other world leaders to readers unknown. Nearby in the Sea of Tranquillity stands a large American flag, its stars and stripes eternally "waving" in a nonexistent breeze, thanks to metal strands that hold the banner upright.

Truly historic events are seldom choreographed in advance, but mankind's first landing on the moon was stage-managed to a fare-thee-well. Before astronaut Armstrong began backing down a short ladder to the lunar surface, he switched on a TV camera to record his descent, and once on the surface, the two Americans' first task was to set up a larger camera that would beam their deeds live to fascinated humans 240,000 miles away.

Impressive stuff. Yet we now view the first landing on the moon through a different lens—a lens of time rather than space. And looking back from our vantage point in 2009, the vaunted Apollo program that brought Americans to the moon can seem more a dead end than a promise of adventures to come. With its lunar mission accomplished, the U.S. had triumphed in its cold war space race with the Soviet Union—and in 1972 NASA ended the Apollo program and turned its sights away from manned missions to the moon.

And that's the pleasure—and utility—of a book like this one: it presents events not in the hurlyburly of real time but from a godlike perspective, thanks to the 20/20 vision of hindsight. From our vantage point in the future, we can look back on the events of 1969 and enjoy seeing which footprints of that remarkable year have endured and which have faded.

Thus, two seemingly minor environment stories of 1969—an oil spill in California and the sudden incineration of an oil-slicked Ohio river—are early indicators of one of today's most pressing issues: mankind's abuse of its home planet. A goofy, silly-season "demonstration" in which a young woman removed her bra outside a department store in California presages the revolution in women's roles that has utterly transformed American society in the 40 years since 1969.

In similar fashion, the coup that put unknown army officer Muammar Gaddafi in charge of Libya served early notice of the emergence of an energetic, newly militant form of Islam that would later assume much more dramatic form in the Tehran hostage crisis of 1979 and the 9/11/01 attacks on the U.S. And a minor altercation between police and patrons of the Stonewall Inn, a gay hangout in New York City's Greenwich Village, gave rise to the Gay Pride movement—and thus to the issue of gay marriage that continues to preoccupy Americans in 2009.

Of course, it isn't news that the cultural divisions in America that first emerged in the 1960s remain the decade's defining legacy. Consider TIME's account of Vice President Spiro Agnew's sharp attacks on antiwar protesters and the media in the fall of 1969: "Armored in the certitudes of middle-class values, he speaks with the authentic voice of Americans who are angry and frightened by what has happened to their culture, who view the '60s as a disastrous montage of pornography, crime, assaults on patriotism, flaming ghettos, marijuana and occupied colleges." Sound familiar? The polarized spectrum of the America we still live in—red state/blue state America—coalesced amid the tie-dyed, trippy days of 1969.

As William Faulkner wrote of the South, "The past isn't dead. It isn't even past." So we hope you enjoy this journey that offers a close encounter not only with our past but also with our present and our future.

—Kelly Knauer

I

Leaps—and Bounds

The ghostly, white-clad figure slowly descended the ladder. Having reached the bottom rung, he lowered himself into the bowl-shaped footpad of *Eagle*, the spindly lunar module of Apollo 11. Then he extended his left foot, cautiously, tentatively, as if testing water in a pool—and, in fact, testing a wholly new environment for man. That groping foot, encased in a heavy, multilayered boot, would remain indelible in the minds of millions who watched it on TV, a symbol of man's determination to step—and forever keep stepping—toward the unknown.

After a few short but interminable seconds, U.S. Astronaut Neil Armstrong placed his foot firmly on the fine-grained surface of the moon. The time was 10:56 p.m. (E.T.), July 20, 1969. Pausing briefly, the first man on the moon spoke the first words uttered on lunar soil: "That's one small step for [a] man, one giant leap for mankind." Seconds later, Edwin "Buzz" Aldrin, right, joined Armstrong on the surface.

With those steps down, the U.S. had stepped up, in magnificent fashion, to meet the challenge issued in 1961 by visionary President John F. Kennedy: to land a man on the moon by the decade's end. Yet in this moment of national triumph, the cheers rang a bit hollow, for the lunar landing came at a time when Americans were deeply divided by a controversial war in Southeast Asia and by a "generation gap" that found young and old citizens squaring off in an angry debate over cultural and political values. The nation's mission in space was accomplished, but the cultural divisions bred in the hothouse of the 1960s remain unresolved, 40 years later.

NASA

BETTMANN CORBIS

A Somber Beginning

On Jan. 20, 1969, the torch of American leadership was passed, as the families of President Lyndon B. Johnson and President-elect Richard M. Nixon gathered on the White House steps prior to Nixon's inauguration. The Republican's victory over Johnson's Vice President, Hubert Humphrey, had capped one of the most remarkable comebacks in U.S. political history. Yet the inaugural day, which often evokes the promise of a fresh start, was unusually restrained. Johnson, one of the most dynamic leaders in U.S. history, had been brought down by the war in Vietnam. And the U.S. was reeling from a hellish year, as TIME's original reporting reveals: "[Americans are] still bewildered by a year of crises hauntingly reminiscent of those that preceded the Civil War and the Depression. As if verging on a national nervous breakdown, the U.S. in 1968 erupted in ghastly events: assassinations, black riots, student protests, rising crime ... why has the can-do country become a country that can't?"

Nixon's Inaugural Address was an evocation of the striving and optimism that are basic to the American temperament: "We have endured a long night of the American spirit. But as our eyes catch the dimness of the first rays of dawn, let us not curse the remaining dark. Let us gather the light." The new President would win re-election in 1972, but when he resigned his office in 1974, the long-sought dawn had not yet broken. His successor, Gerald Ford, would say upon Nixon's parting: "Our long national nightmare is over."

5

HUBERT VAN ES—AP IMAGES

For a Wounded Nation, No Exit

The soldiers at left, from the U.S. Army's 101st Airborne Division, are carrying a comrade from an evacuation helicopter to receive medical care. But for the nation they served, there was no deus ex machina in sight. The Vietnam War, which had begun as a smallish cold war mission in a little-known, faraway land, had metastasized into a cancer that afflicted the entire nation, shredding the military, dividing America's house at home and tarnishing its image abroad. President Lyndon Johnson, who had ordered the massive escalation that by 1969 found 537,500 U.S. troops in Southeast Asia, had been swallowed up in the quicksand and did not seek re-election. With the inauguration of Richard Nixon, Americans devoutly hoped for a change of course in the war.

The honeymoon was brief, as TIME reported in its March 16 issue: "The war in Vietnam remains an inexorable burden ... For Richard Nixon, who entered office amid new hopes that peace might not be far off and that Ho Chi Minh might finally be amenable to agreement, that discovery was not long in coming. Last week continued Communist attacks in South Vietnam ... jeopardized the climate of calm and unity that [Nixon] had worked so hard to create. The attacks left 453 Americans dead in the first week, a higher toll than for any one week since last May—higher even than in the first full week of the Tet offensive a year ago." Americans now used a single, devastating word for the war: quagmire.

Wider Protests Against the War

The year 1969 began amid hopes that the nation's new President, Richard Nixon, might have a solution for America's most anguishing problem, the deep quagmire in Vietnam. It was now four years since President Lyndon Johnson had launched the massive buildup in U.S. troops in Southeast Asia, and though Nixon did begin drawing down troop levels in the summer, by the fall there was no sign that a turning point in the war was in sight. Antiwar activists responded by calling for two massive protests, a nationwide Moratorium Day against the war on Oct. 15 and a "Mobilization" march on Washington on Nov. 15.

October's Moratorium brought hundreds of thousands into streets across the country, with the largest turnouts, predictably, in cities with large student populations. Some 100,000 people attended a rally in Boston; 45,000 joined a candlelight march on the White House in Washington; 20,000 gathered on Wall Street in New York City. Sentiment against the protests, TIME reported, was strongest in the Midwest and South; even so, in Memphis, only 37 people attended a patriotic rally organized by a police lieutenant. At right, a scene from November's huge march in the capital; above, protesters square off with U.S. Army troops outside Fort Dix in New Jersey during October's Moratorium demonstrations.

8

All You Need Is Hate

He seemed to spring full-blown from America's darkest nightmares, the embodiment of every middle-class fear about the values—or lack of values—of the youthful counterculture. But if Charles Manson used drugs, sex and rock 'n' roll as aids in exerting control over his "family" of gullible young misfits, he represented a type that recurs with alarming regularity in history: the charismatic cult leader whose pleasure consists in toying with the submissiveness of his flock of followers. He claimed to draw inspiration from the Beatles, dubbing his war on society "Helter Skelter," after one of the British group's more frenetic rockers, but Manson was about as far from the band's peace-and-love message as it is possible to get. His true compatriots are Rasputin, Mao Zedong and Jim Jones.

The gruesome series of senseless murders that brought Manson the notoriety he craved began on Aug. 9, when four of his deluded followers headed into the hills of Los Angeles, heeding his order: "Society has wronged me. We'll kill whatever pigs are in that house. Go in there and get them." The details of the revolting butchery of five victims that followed—and of the two additional murders committed by Manson's devotees the next night—shocked the nation. Yet Los Angeles detectives bungled the case; it was not until Dec. 9 that Manson, then residing in an Independence, Calif., jail cell facing charges of car theft, was brought to the city, right, to face trial for engineering the murder spree.

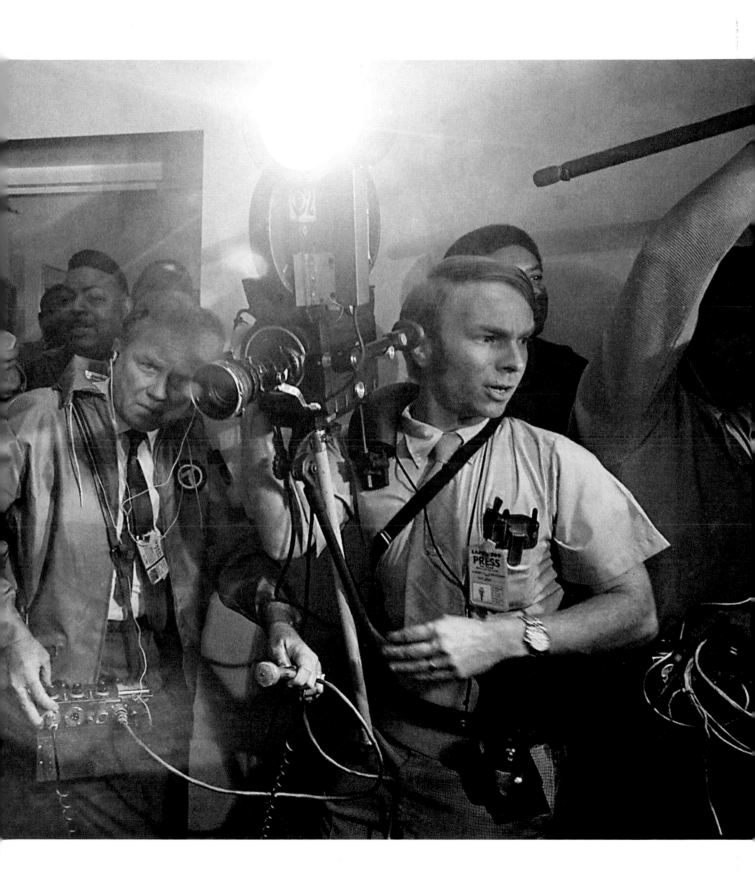

Party of the Decade

When 400,000 grooving hippies descended on Max Yasgur's farm in upstate New York and partied their way through what Time described as "history's biggest happening," even the sober-sided weekly magazine, the voice of the American establishment, caught a contact high. "As the moment when the special culture of U.S. youth of the '60s openly displayed its strength, appeal and power, [Woodstock] may well rank as one of the significant political and sociological events of the age," Time opined. "The lure of the festival was an all-star cast of top rock artists … But the good vibrations turned out to be the least of it … Thousands of young people, who had previously thought of themselves as part of an isolated minority, experienced the euphoric

sense of discovering that they are, as the saying goes, what's happening."

Ouch. Yes, we know: TIME wasn't exactly hip in the 1960s. But like everyone else who made the pilgrimage to Yasgur's farm and watched gifted guitarist Carlos Santana and his group rock the house, above, TIME understood that the "euphoric sense" of the event originated in large part from the marijuana that was openly smoked by the attendees, and the magazine wondered how long "the nation's present laws against its use can remain in force without seeming as absurd and hypocritical as Prohibition." Forty years later, the battle over legalizing pot goes on, proving that TIME in 1969 was not only unhip—it was also no great shakes at prognostication.

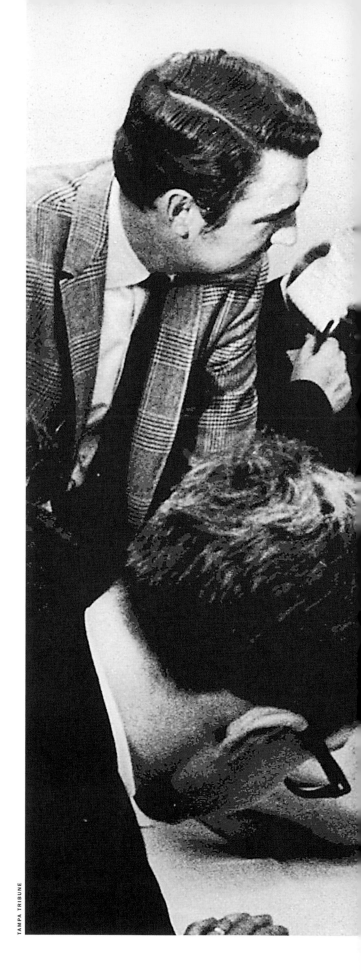

He Came, He Jawed, He Conquered

In 1969, Americans were just getting used to a new method of determining the pro football championship—the grandly titled Super Bowl matchup between the top teams in the newly united National Football League, which merged the venerable NFL with the upstart American Football League into a new super-league with two conferences. But those who tuned in saw a historic game, as quarterback Joe Namath of the nine-year-old New York Jets single-handedly turned the third meeting between the pro game's rival divisions into the year's most exciting sporting event. That single hand, of course, was "Broadway Joe's" right hand; his spot-on, 17-for-28 passing picked apart the defense of the lordly Baltimore Colts as the Jets beat them 16-7 on Jan. 12. At right, Joe savors his historic victory.

Yet it wasn't just the upset that turned Namath into a legend at the ripe old age of 26: it was the setup for the upset. For Joe was a loudmouth, a hot dog, a preening, cocky kid who in a Holly-wood film would likely be taught a lesson by the older, more experienced Colts. Before the game, when the only slim hopes the Jets had of winning centered on Namath's arm, the only thing he seemed to be exercising was his mouth. Holding court at poolside or swirling a double Scotch-on-the-rocks at a pregame banquet, his message was always the same: "We're gonna win. I guarantee it." Joe kept his promise, serving notice that both the AFC and the Super Bowl were here to stay.

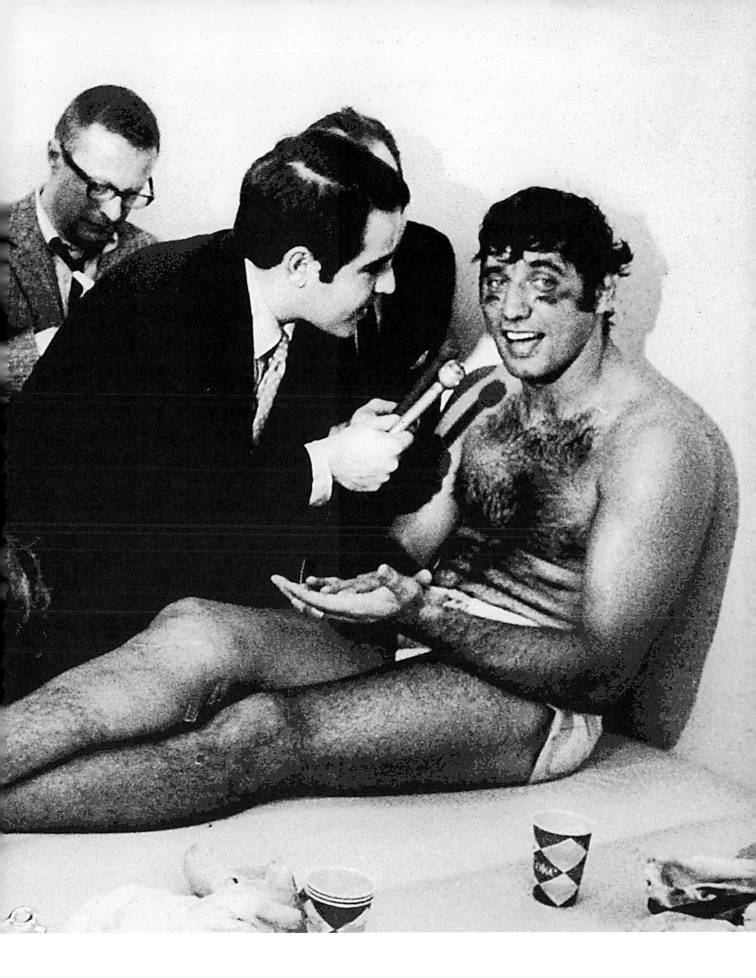

A Day in the Life

Reality check: it was the night of Feb. 9, 1964, when the Beatles first appeared on Ed Sullivan's TV show and began their conquest of America. If their publicity-friendly pudding-bowl haircuts created a sensation back then, look what five years of immersion in the white-hot crucible of the 1960s had done to the group's most rebellious member, John Lennon. June of 1969 found the rocker and his new wife, Japanese avant-garde artist Yoko Ono, ensconced in a Montreal hotel room, engaged in the sort of high-concept hijinks that defined the period: a "bed-in for peace."

Restless within the unfriendly confines of pop stardom, Lennon explored psychedelic drugs and Transcendental Meditation with his bandmates. But it wasn't until he hooked up with Ono that he found the new persona he had been seeking. After his divorce from wife Cynthia early in 1969, John and Yoko turned their lives into performance art, Ono's specialty, merging their artistic, musical, personal and political fixations into a flamboyant, provocative traveling circus.

A slice of their lifestyle is glimpsed at right: joined by rebel comedian Tommy Smothers and LSD guru Timothy Leary and his wife Rosemary, John and Yoko run through his latest song—he had come to view his songs as newspapers, he said, and indeed that spring's Beatles hit *The Ballad of John and Yoko* was essentially a bulletin from the front lines of his life. Yet amid all the hoopla, Lennon remained a brilliant artist and polemicist: the antiwar song recorded in this room became an anthem of nonviolence whose power has never dated. "All we are saying," he is singing, "is give peace a chance."

WAR'S BITTER HARVEST *Above, a wounded U.S. paratrooper grimaces in pain as he awaits evacuation from "Hamburger Hill" in May. At right, a helicopter brings supplies to U.S. troops atop the battered, bombed-out peak christened "Bunker Hill" in March*

Churning in a Quagmire

For Americans, 1969 was another year of frustration in Vietnam

EBRUARY 23, 1969. ALL ACROSS THEIR WAR-WEARY land, South Vietnamese were sleeping off the revelry of Tet, Vietnam's happiest festival. This year's Tet had passed peacefully, unlike the nightmare of 1968, when some 200,000 North Vietnamese Army and Viet Cong fighters smashed into South Vietnam's cities and towns. Then, at 2 a.m., in a whoosh of rockets and thud of mortars, the nightmare began again. Barely 19 hours after they had ended a self-imposed, week-long Tet truce, enemy gunners launched coordinated rocket and mortar attacks on more than 100 cities, towns and military installations throughout South Vietnam, including the capital of Saigon.

This time, at least in the first phases of the attacks, the North Vietnamese and Viet Cong appeared to be aiming primarily at military targets, not civilians.

However, several Soviet-built 122-mm rockets fell into Saigon, killing at least six civilians—the first such bombardment of South Vietnamese civilian areas since President Lyndon Johnson ordered a bombing halt over North Vietnam on Oct. 31, 1968. Danang, the country's second largest city, suffered greater damage. Rockets and mortar rounds poured into the city as well as into surrounding military installations, while infiltrating communist infantry prowled the streets.

Other attacks shook the imperial city of Hué, Pleiku in the Central Highlands and the sprawling supply base at Cam Ranh Bay. Long Binh, a U.S. headquarters and logistics base just north of Saigon, was hit by 80 mortar rounds and a number of rockets. The communists appeared to be violating the tacit understanding that Johnson thought he had reached with Hanoi when he

PEAK EFFORT *On May 21, after a 10-day assault, victorious U.S. troops occupy the top of battle-scarred "Hamburger Hill"*

ordered the bombing halt: in return, the communists would withdraw troops from the Demilitarized Zone separating North and South Vietnam, begin serious negotiations in Paris—and end the shelling of major population centers. Clearly, the North Vietnamese were testing new U.S. President Richard Nixon. He responded the next month by ordering the secret bombing of North Vietnamese sanctuaries in Cambodia.

The Tet attacks left 453 Americans dead in the first week, bringing the total number of U.S. dead in Vietnam to 32,376. It was an omen of the year to come: just as this Tet offensive seemed a bitter replay of the 1968 version, so 1969 would be a replay of the past few years, with the U.S. and its South Vietnamese allies unable to make progress, either on the battlefield or in bringing North Vietnam closer to ending the war.

ON THE MILITARY FRONT, THE POST-TET ATTACKS and a second onslaught unleashed by North Vietnam in August were the most important actions of 1969. Indeed, for much of the year, the war's key fronts seemed far from the fighting: in the conference rooms of Paris, in the council rooms of Washington, in the streets where Americans marched in protest, vowing to "bring the war home."

In Washington, President Nixon soon learned that the Paris peace talks with North Vietnam, where delegates were arguing over whether the deliberating table should be round or rectangular, held little promise of a breakthrough. Yet he was determined to change the tempo of events and show Americans he was committed to drawing down the U.S. presence in South Vietnam. After a meeting with South Vietnam's President, Nguyen Van Thieu, at Midway Island, Nixon surprised Americans on June 8 by announcing that he would unilaterally draw down the number of U.S. troops in Vietnam by 25,000 by late August, leaving some 512,000 U.S. troops on the ground in South Vietnam.

When word reached the troops chosen to depart first, TIME reported, "green second lieutenants and combat-toughened veterans ran through their unit areas, shouting and weeping for joy at the realization that, for them at least, the war would soon be over." Nixon upped the ante in September, saying he would withdraw another 35,000 troops, reducing the total to well below 500,000. The moves focused concern on the policy he hoped would ultimately end the U.S. commitment: Vietnamization, by which U.S. forces would train South Vietnamese soldiers to take their place.

With Congress, the President also acted to remove inequities in the nation's Selective Service system, ending deferments that sheltered college students and put

TICKET HOME *On Aug. 27, 1969, troops of the U.S. 9th Infantry Division line up to fly to Hawaii and then back to the U.S.*

the burden of service on the poor and minorities. On Dec. 1, a nationally televised lottery allotted priority in the draft based on one's day of birth as selected in a random drawing. It was a grim metaphor for the war: a possible death sentence handed by the old to the young with all the majesty of a bingo game.

ONE MEMORABLE BATTLE CAME TO STAND FOR THE state of the U.S. war effort in 1969. On May 10, nine battalions of American and Vietnamese troops were airlifted into landing zones near Ap Bia, a.k.a Hill 937, a mountain in South Vietnam's A Shau Valley. Their mission: shut down an infiltration route used by North Vietnamese forces. There was little contact at first, but the next day, members of the U.S. 101st Airborne Division surprised a North Vietnamese trail-watching squad and wiped it out. Estimating that a company of North Vietnamese occupied the hill (it turned out to be part of two regiments), U.S. officers ordered an attack on the peak on May 12. The troopers quickly ran into "garbage": rocket grenades, fire from automatic weapons, lethal Claymore mines dangling from bushes and trees. They pulled back. An assault by two companies on May 13 was also repulsed by the North Vietnamese. On May 14 the Americans charged again and nearly made the top of the hill, but the attack

petered out. Reinforcements were brought up, and on May 18, two battalions tried again and were thrown back just short of the crest in a blinding rainstorm and a shower of communist grenades. By now the grunts had a new name for Hill 937: "Hamburger Hill."

Two days later, on May 20, after more than 20,000 artillery rounds and 155 air strikes had virtually denuded the top of Hill 937, the U.S. assault force finally took the peak. The price: 84 heroic soldiers dead and 480 more wounded. The U.S. command claimed that 622 North Vietnamese had been killed, though only 182 weapons were found, calling the death count into question.

Then, only a week later, came the blow: the U.S. gave up control of the hill and withdrew. When Americans at home expressed their dismay, Army brass called the battle a "tremendous, gallant victory" and explained that their aim, as always in the long war, had been not to seize ground but to disperse or destroy the enemy. But more and more Americans, both at home and in Vietnam, were asking the question TIME corrrespondent John Wilhelm found on a piece of cardboard with a black 101st Airborne neckerchief attached, pinned by a G.I. knife to a blackened tree trunk. "Hamburger Hill," a soldier had scrawled on the cardboard, and someone else had added the words, "Was it worth it?"

Images of Vietnam

Combat photographers risked their lives to capture indelible images of a brutal war in a faraway land

GRENADE TOSS *Noted* LIFE *photographer Larry Burrows took the picture above of U.S. and South Vietnamese soldiers firing on an enemy position in 1969. Late in the year, President Richard Nixon announced he would pursue a policy of "Vietnamizing" the war by assigning most combat to South Vietnam's army and drawing down the number of U.S. troops*

IN COUNTRY *At right, soldiers from the U.S. Army 9th Infantry Division wade across a stream in the Mekong Delta, about 45 miles southwest of Saigon, in June*

RETURN *Exhausted G.I.s of the U.S. 9th Infantry Division relax on the boat trip home after a daylong foray in the Mekong Delta*

AHHH! *A U.S. soldier enjoys using a stream in the Mekong Delta to cool off and clean his weapon. Vietnam was the first major war in which the U.S. Army was fully integrated*

PALS *Lieutenant John Kerry relaxes with "VC" aboard* PCF-94 *in 1969, the year he was awarded a Purple Heart, his second, for a leg wound, and a Silver Star for valor in action*

AT EASE *Troopers from the 1st Air Cavalry Division grab some sun in the Dau Tieng district of Binh Duong Province*

MOVING IN *On March 4, 1969, troopers from the 1st Cavalry Division race between rubber trees during an assault on a Viet Cong bunker complex inside the Michelin rubber plantation, in the Dau Tieng district of southeast South Vietnam*

IN CHARGE *Captain Larry Buts leads a pack of Hurricane Aircats up the Mekong Delta. His force included Chinese mercenaries*

APOCALYPSE THEN *Stars and Stripes unfurled, a U.S. patrol boat heads up the Mekong River outside the regional capital, My Tho. "The war of misty beginnings seems to lack an end,"* TIME *observed in March 1969. "Just who is the enemy, anyway?"*

MEDIC! *U.S. 101st Airborne Division troopers evacuate a wounded comrade during the battle for Hamburger Hill in May 1969*

Nixon Takes the Helm

A new President aims for consensus but settles for division

I ASK YOU TO JOIN IN A HIGH ADVENTURE—ONE AS RICH as humanity itself, and as exciting as the times we live in," Richard Nixon declared to Americans and the world in the closing words of his Inaugural Address in January 1969. But the new President and his staff soon discovered that while the Oval Office offered no shortage of adventure and excitement, it was seldom of the kind they wished for. Nixon inherited a world of woes from the exhausted Johnson Administration. Abroad, the U.S. faced an enormous challenge in Vietnam, cold war tensions with the Soviet Union and China, a Middle East poised on the brink of new war and European allies estranged by U.S. policy in Vietnam. And the home front, rent by dissension, seemed at times as if it were alien territory to Nixon; he and his team grappled with its complexities only grudgingly.

Two weeks after taking office, Nixon scribbled notes to himself before an interview with TIME's longtime White House correspondent, Hugh Sidey, that reveal how he wished to be perceived: "Compassionate, Bold, New, Courageous … Zest for the job (not lonely but awesome) … Idea magnet … Mrs. RN—glamour, dignity … Open Channels for Dissent … Progress—Participation, Trustworthy, Open-minded. Need to be good to do good … The nation must be better in spirit at the end of the term. Need for joy, serenity, confidence, inspiration."

This kaleidoscope of images and ideas provides insight into the mind of the man who occupied the Oval Office in 1969: restless, highly intelligent, complicated and more than a little calculating. The new President represented the moderate, Eastern wing of the Republican Party, which would later turn to the more conservative, Western-oriented politics of Ronald Reagan. And it showed: especially during his first year in office, Nixon was seldom driven by ideology. Instead, his approach was improvisational and sometimes contradictory, often opportunistic and always pragmatic.

All these qualities were in evidence in his first major policy initiative, which took place largely in secret. With a handful of top aides, Nixon began slowly preparing both the government and the public for a change in strategy toward Mao Zedong's communist China. The Administration started easing travel restrictions and trade barriers, while Nixon's powerful National Security Adviser, Henry Kissinger, began signaling to Beijing via back-door channels that the U.S. was newly receptive to exploring direct contact.

These initiatives would culminate, years later, in Nixon's crowning achievement: the opening of diplomatic relations with China. But for now, they took place almost entirely out of public view. As Nixon knew, China and the Soviet Union were engaged in a series of violent border clashes in 1969. Nixon believed—correctly, as it turned out—that playing China and Russia against each other would draw both into a closer relationship with the U.S. He appears also to have hoped that it

SWORN IN *After his inauguration, the 37th President shakes hands with campaign adversary Hubert Humphrey, while notables including congressional GOP leaders Gerald Ford and Everett Dirksen, the Rev. Billy Graham and new V.P. Spiro Agnew look on*

HELLO, BERLIN *After only five weeks in the presidency, Nixon visited five European capitals on a goodwill tour, hoping to mend alliances rent by Vietnam. The trip was a success; in Berlin, above,* TIME *reported that "the crowd was ... wildly enthusiastic"*

FEEDBACK *After he called on "the silent majority" for support in November, Nixon was deluged with positive mail*

would compel them to decrease their support for North Vietnam, but on this score he was wrong.

Hoping to patch up America's frayed relations with key European allies, Nixon embarked on a tour of five European capitals in late February, assuring leaders abroad that the U.S. would no longer neglect them. Presenting himself as a moderate who would "seek to consult, not to convince," he was received well. "Richard Nixon is underwhelming Europe, and the Europeans seem rather grateful," reported TIME's Sidey.

From early on, Nixon began to show the penchant for secret dealings that would ultimately bring down his presidency. In March, he secretly ordered his generals to begin bombing sections of the Ho Chi Minh Trail that zigzagged through Cambodia. When a reporter for the New York *Times* broke the story months later, an infuriated Nixon secretly ordered the FBI to begin tapping the phones of several Defense Department employees and White House staffers he suspected of leaking the news. At the same time, Nixon publicly moved to undercut domestic opposition to the war by announcing that some 10% of all U.S. troops fighting in Vietnam would be coming home by year's end.

Nixon showed a surer hand in foreign policy by refusing to escalate a potential crisis after North Korea shot down a U.S. spy plane on April 15, killing 31 U.S. servicemen. In the Middle East, America's friendship with Israel led to considerable hand-wringing (again, behind closed doors) over reports by U.S. intelligence agencies that the Jewish state was building a nuclear arsenal. When Israel's new Prime Minister, Golda Meir, visited the White House in September, the two apparently came to a private understanding: the U.S. would stop pressing Tel Aviv to submit to nuclear inspections and sign the Nonproliferation Treaty, while Israel, in turn, would refrain from the use of nuclear weapons and would never admit that it possessed them.

If he moved aggressively to play an active role abroad, Nixon was less engaged at home. "I've always thought the country could run itself domestically without a President," Nixon once said to LIFE's Theodore H. White—a notion that might have been true in

"Let us understand: North Vietnam cannot defeat or humiliate the United States. Only Americans can do that."

—RICHARD NIXON

times of prosperity and amity but only revealed his distance from the roiling, contentious energies at loose in America's streets. Even so, he quickly showed he was anything but an ideologue on domestic policy.

In the first days of the new Administration, Attorney General (and close Nixon adviser) John Mitchell counseled observers to "watch what we do, not what we say." Sure enough, Nixon often offered rhetorical support to the right while actually tracking toward liberals on policy. He moved in his first year to create not only the Environmental Protection Agency but also the Occupational Safety and Health Administration.

The President also implemented a series of groundbreaking racial quotas and preferences, the Philadelphia Plan, and pushed for a Family Assistance Plan (the brainchild of his domestic adviser, Harvard professor Daniel Patrick Moynihan) that would have guaranteed a minimum annual income for families on wel-

fare. Both liberals and conservatives were stunned by Nixon's support for the idea. He similarly shocked both sides of the aisle when his concerns about inflation (and unemployment, which tracked upward later in the year) led him to become the first Republican President to endorse deficit spending as a means to stimulate the economy.

YET NIXON'S EARLY OVERTURES TO THE LEFT WERE rebuffed. His decision to bring home troops from Vietnam was assailed as too little, too late by Democrats in Congress, who had happily agreed to every escalation of the war demanded by Kennedy and Johnson. And the Family Assistance Plan was smothered in its crib by liberals who felt it was not generous enough. Nixon's stated desire to govern from the center, at least at the start of his Administration, was probably genuine. But it was also unrealistic, coming amid one of

ALOHA! *The Nixon family stops over in Hawaii in June 1969, as the President traveled to Midway Island to meet with South Vietnam's leaders. David Eisenhower, grandson of the former President, and Julie Nixon, in yellow, were married in December 1968, just before Nixon became President. Older daughter Tricia would marry Edward Cox at the White House in 1971*

MEET THE NEW BOSS *Nixon was hailed by U.S. troops when he paid a surprise visit to South Vietnam in July 1969*

the most divisive decades in U.S. history. Nor could the new President ignore the right flank, whose support had brought him to the White House: among his first acts was the nomination of conservative federal judge Warren Burger as Chief Justice of the Supreme Court, to replace the retiring Earl Warren. Burger took office in June with the avowed goal of rolling back many of the Warren Court's liberal reforms.

EARLY ON, NIXON HAD HOPED TO PRESENT HIM-self as one who could "open channels for dissent." But by the fall, unable to win over his critics and sensing the American public was on his side, he decided instead to open fire on the dissenters. On Nov. 3, midway between the massive Moratorium and Mobilization antiwar protests, he went on television to appeal "to you, the great silent majority of my fellow Americans. I ask for your support ... Let us be united for peace. Let us also be united against defeat. Because let us understand: North Vietnam cannot defeat or humiliate the United States. Only Americans can do that." It was a masterly ploy, with the President ostensibly appealing for patriotism, calm and reason while actually stoking the worst fears of his supporters and driving

his opponents into a frenzy of rage and distraction.

Ten days later, Nixon unleashed his Administration's pit bull, Vice President Spiro Agnew, to launch a full-bore attack on the academics and media the White House felt were poisoning public opinion. Railing against the "tiny and closed fraternity of privileged men" who decided what was news and university protesters who were taught nonsense by "an effete corps of impudent snobs," Agnew gave a series of tough-talking speeches that polarized the nation. The attacks revealed that Nixon, the new custodian of America's divided house, had now decided to widen its divisions.

Yet behind the bluster, Nixon harbored private doubts. A week before his "silent majority" speech, he asked Kissinger, "Is it possible we were wrong from the start in Vietnam?" Desperate to change the narrative in Southeast Asia, he tried using both the carrot and the stick. At times, he played the tough guy: "I want the North Vietnamese to believe," he told his chief of staff, Bob Haldeman, "that I've reached the point that I might do anything to stop the war. We'll just slip the word to them that for God's sake, you know 'Nixon is obsessed about communism. We can't restrain him when he's angry, and he has his hand on the nuclear button'—and [North Vietnamese leader] Ho Chi Minh himself will be in Paris in two days begging for peace." In October, Nixon secretly ordered U.S. nuclear forces worldwide to go to a heightened state of alert.

Nixon's ploy failed to move the North Vietnamese, who remained unwilling to reach an agreement in Paris. Now Nixon turned to the carrot, playing the role of peacemaker. On Nov. 25, he announced that the U.S. would renounce the possession and use of deadly biological weapons, even for retaliatory purposes, and would destroy its entire stockpile of biological weapons over the next few years. That same month, he put new stress on the policy of "Vietnamization"—a plan to turn ground combat over to South Vietnamese troops as U.S. servicemen were brought home. The proposal failed to move the North Vietnamese or to mollify anti-war protesters on America's college campuses.

"The nation must be better in spirit at the end of the term. Need for joy, serenity, confidence, inspiration," Nixon had reminded himself early in 1969. Eleven months later, hundreds of thousands of Americans were marching outside the White House to protest the war, while Nixon was calling for unity on one hand and ordering his minions to stoke the fires of division on the other. Both the nation and the President were back where they had started the year: still sorely in need of joy, serenity, confidence and inspiration.

INNER SANCTUM *Nixon meets with Haldeman, economic aide Donald Rumsfeld (who would serve as Secretary of Defense under George W. Bush) and Ehrlichman in the Oval Office in 1969*

Life in the Bubble: The Nixon White House
A "Berlin Wall" of confidants restricted access to the President

LIKE MANY PRESIDENTS BEFORE HIM, RICHARD Nixon took office vowing he would remain in close touch with the American people. Yet he seemed happy to remain inside the "bubble" that famously surrounds the office. His personal penchant for secrecy and privacy, magnified by his fear of staff leaks to the media, isolated him to an unusual degree. Critics in Washington soon began complaining that access to Nixon was controlled by a "palace guard" headed by chief of staff H.R. (Bob) Haldeman, domestic adviser John Ehrlichman and the powerful national security adviser Henry Kissinger *(see following page).*

"The Teutonic trio is now known as 'the Berlin Wall' in the White House pressroom," TIME reported. "One Administration official calls them 'all the king's Krauts' ... Haldeman and Ehrlichman are widely called 'Von Haldeman' and 'Von Ehrlichman'—or simply 'the Germans.'" The two men screened nearly every person admitted to the President's lair and practically every piece of paper that reached his desk or briefcase. While Lyndon Johnson had proudly shown visitors his 60-button telephone console, Nixon had just three direct lines—to Haldeman, Ehrlichman and Kissinger.

A fourth insider, Attorney General John Mitchell, was not part of the White House staff but was one of the President's closest confidants. Their intimacy dated back to their days as law partners in New York City. Mitchell, 55 in 1969, had served ably as Nixon's campaign manager in the 1968 election.

Haldeman, 43 in 1969, was a longtime advertising executive who first worked as an advance man for Nixon's 1956 vice-presidential campaign. The "city manager of the White House," an insider told TIME, was the enforcer who saw that things got done.

Ehrlichman, 44 in 1969, rose swiftly under Nixon. He began as White House counsel and troubleshooter—policing conflicts of interest on the staff, working up legislation, managing Nixon's financial affairs. But when Nixon's two top domestic advisers didn't see eye to eye, he put Ehrlichman, a lawyer who had toiled on his campaigns since 1960, above them, the domestic equivalent of foreign-affairs maestro Kissinger.

Nixon's first love was Kissinger's portfolio. "The old man," a Nixon aide told TIME, "doesn't give a damn about parks and stuff ... He's not interested in mobile homes or farm problems. He wants to talk to Henry Kissinger about foreign policy, and he expects the Germans to keep people away from him so he can do it."

While Kissinger was not involved in the Watergate scandal that led to Nixon's resignation in 1974, the other three men were tarred. Haldeman was found guilty of conspiracy and obstruction of justice; Ehrlichman of conspiracy, obstruction of justice and perjury. Each served 18 months in prison. Mitchell was found guilty of conspiracy, obstruction of justice and perjury, and he served 19 months. The former Attorney General died in 1988, Haldeman in 1993, Ehrlichman in 1999.

HENRY THE FIRST *With his Germanic accent and outsized opinion of himself, Kissinger was both respected and lampooned by Americans in 1969—and he probably approved when noted* TIME-LIFE *photographer Alfred Eisenstaedt gave him a halo*

Henry Kissinger

A Harvard professor changes the balance of power in the White House

"H E IS NOT EXACTLY A HOUSEHOLD NAME," *TIME* declared of President Richard Nixon's National Security Adviser, Harvard professor Henry Kissinger, weeks into the new Administration. But within months, Kissinger had become one of the most famous people in America, and the question in Washington was no longer whether Kissinger would have Nixon's ear—but whether he would ever relinquish it. From Nixon's first days in office, Kissinger and his top-notch staff began grinding out position papers from their basement quarters in the West Wing that quickly dominated the strategic direction of U.S. foreign policy.

Like President Eisenhower, who changed the model for all future Administrations when he installed a military-style chief of staff system to run the West Wing, President Nixon forever changed the balance of power in U.S. administrations by elevating the formerly junior role of National Security Adviser to become the leading strategic voice on foreign policy in the White House, often outranking the Secretary of State.

Kissinger ran with the assignment. "Humility is not his hallmark," TIME observed of the academic, then 45, who had served as an adviser to three previous Administrations. Describing Kissinger as composed and inconspicuous in appearance, the magazine noted that he had been working 18-hour days since taking his new position, that his new bachelor quarters in the capital were a shambles (he and his first wife had divorced in 1964) and that he had a reputation for being brusque with colleagues, students and office help.

The German-born Jew, whose family had managed to immigrate to America in 1938, served in Europe as a U.S. Army interpreter during World War II, then became a distinguished academic specializing in foreign policy. Now the student of statecraft was tutoring America's top statesman in the Oval Office. "There cannot be a crisis next week," Kissinger advised TIME. "My schedule is already full."

ALFRED EISENSTAEDT—TIME LIFE PICTURES

Spiro Agnew

As "Nixon's Nixon," he gave voice to the fears of Middle Americans

THE VICE PRESIDENT OF THE UNITED STATES IS traditionally almost a non-person in Washington," TIME observed in its Nov. 14, 1969, issue. "Spiro Theodore Agnew, however, is turning the vice-presidency into something like an oratorical happening, raising the No. 2 office to a level of visibility and controversy unknown since the days of, well, Richard Nixon. Agnew is not merely seeking political capital in the South, nor is his rhetoric aimed only at Moratorium marchers and other opponents of the war. Rather, he is emerging as a kind of improbable mahdi of Middle America ... Armored in the certitudes of middle-class values, he speaks with the authentic voice of Americans who are angry and frightened by what has happened to their culture, who view the '60s as a disastrous montage of pornography, crime, assaults on patriotism, flaming ghettos, marijuana and occupied colleges. If he speaks with Richard Nixon's tacit approval—and he does—Agnew does his duty gladly, bringing missionary zeal and a sense of moral outrage to his oratory ... in effect, Agnew is acting as Nixon's Nixon ... flailing at 'ideological eunuchs,' 'merchants of hate,' 'parasites of passion' and campus protesters who 'take their tactics from Castro and their money from Daddy.'"

Agnew's exhortations, usually the work of White House speechwriters William Safire and Patrick Buchanan, often rose to lofty heights of scorn. Speaking in New Orleans in the fall of 1969, he memorably excoriated war protesters: "A spirit of masochism prevails, encouraged by an effete corps of impudent snobs who characterize themselves as intellectuals." California pollster Mervin Field told TIME, "Agnew is strumming a real gut chord" with such attacks.

Yet if his words resonated, Agnew's frequent slips of the tongue when off-script often damaged the White House. In 1969 he referred to Poles as "Polacks" and noted, "If you've seen one slum, you've seen them all." Even so, Nixon kept Agnew as his running mate in 1972. In October 1973, Agnew was charged with having accepted bribes while holding office as Baltimore County Executive, as Governor of Maryland and as Vice President. He agreed to plead no contest to a single charge that he had failed to report $29,500 in income in 1967 and to resign the office of Vice President. In a 1980 book, Agnew claimed he had been innocent but resigned under pressure from Nixon. He died in 1996.

ASSAULT BY ALLITERATION *In 1970, Agnew would dismiss the mainstream media as "nattering nabobs of negativism"*

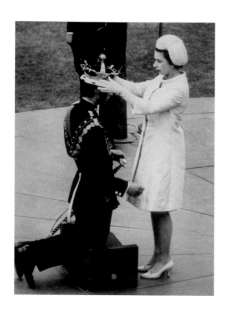

The Man Who Would Be King

A Prince of Wales is crowned, with pomp and circumstance

ALAS FOR THE HEIR APPARENT TO THE CROWN OF Britain! As the young man approached his 21st birthday, the reigning monarch, Queen Elizabeth II, noted that her son, H.R.H. Prince Charles Philip Arthur George Mountbatten-Windsor, Prince of Wales, Earl of Chester, Duke of Cornwall in the peerage of England; Duke of Rothesay, Earl of Carrick, and Lord of Renfrew in the peerage of Scotland; Lord of the Isles and Great Steward of Scotland, was alarmingly deficient in regal headwear. And so a date was set: on July 1, 1969, Charles would be crowned in his most august role, the one accorded the heir apparent since 1301, after the British conquest of the Welsh: Prince of Wales.

And so it was that on the appointed day, the royal carriage procession jogged through the streets of Caernarfon in Wales to the Water Gate set in the limestone walls of the city's ancient castle. When Charles arrived, the state trumpeters of the Household Cavalry sounded a fanfare. His personal banner, carrying the arms of Llywelyn the Great with the coronet of the Prince of Wales in the center, was broken out over the castle's Eagle Tower. Then Charles was conducted by Lord Snowdon,

the Constable of the Castle, to the Chamberlain Tower, while the assemblage sang *God Bless the Prince of Wales.*

Now the Queen arrived and directed that the Prince be summoned. Charles, whom TIME described as "a pleasant, jug-eared young man of 20 who likes to fly planes, drive sports cars, play the trumpet and the cello, and who once delivered a very creditable Macbeth on a school stage," approached, wearing an ermine-trimmed velvet mantle over his blue uniform as Colonel-in-Chief of the Royal Regiment of Wales. As he knelt before Elizabeth, the letters patent of investiture were read, first in English, then in Welsh. (The Welsh rendition was an innovation aimed at placating Welsh tribal sensibilities.) The Queen then presented Charles with a sword, placed a coronet on his head, slipped a gold ring on his finger and handed him a gold rod of government. Thus accoutered, Charles knelt before the Queen and repeated the ancient oath of his unique profession: "I, Charles, Prince of Wales, do become your liege man of life and limb and of earthly worship, and faith and truth I will bear unto you to live and die against all manner of folks." Done! And so to bed.

H.R.H. *Above, the official portrait of the Prince of Wales. At left, the investiture ceremony, and* TIME'S *June 27, 1969, cover, painted by ur-'60s designer Peter Max. Charles, who has always shown a refreshing sense of humor about his royal role, told* TIME, *"I think it's something that dawns on you with the most ghastly, inexorable sense. I didn't suddenly wake up in my pram one day and say 'Yippee,' you know."*

Tensions and Transitions
New leaders take the stage, and old woes beset Northern Ireland

NORTHERN IRELAND ERUPTS *"The six Ulster counties that form Northern Ireland shuddered on the edge of civil war last week,"* TIME *reported in its May 2, 1969, issue. "Nearly every city and town was divided into two armed camps, as fanatic Protestants and rebellious Catholics faced each other down, ready to do street battle with stones, staves and worse. Skillful saboteurs triggered three explosions that cut Belfast's water supply in half. Post offices and a bus station were set aflame by fire bombs; police stations were stoned ... More than 1,000 British soldiers moved into position throughout Ulster to protect reservoirs, telephone exchanges and power stations."* The firestorm between angry Roman Catholics (shown above, manning barricades) and pro-British Protestant storm troopers loyal to the firebrand Rev. Ian Paisley flared through the rest of the year. By August, Britain sent 6,500 troops to Belfast and Londonderry to keep the peace. "The Troubles," as the Irish called their home-grown religious war, would not be resolved for decades—and in March 2009, a flurry of attacks on British troops still patrolling Northern Ireland served notice that the "Good Friday" peace pact reached in 1998 might not last.

SHOCK TROOPS *Alas for China's huddled masses: they were still yearning to breathe free in 1969, three years after Chairman Mao Zedong unleashed the Great Proletarian Cultural Revolution, a reign of chaos that turned his people into paranoid, starving pawns in a vast political game. At right, rural workers pose for a propaganda photo reading Mao's* Little Red Book. *The chalkboard informs us they are "celebrating the opening of the 9th Party Congress." Noted. Meanwhile, on China's border with the U.S.S.R., battles broke out along disputed areas. The bonds that once united the world's two communist giants would never be restored.*

A NEW LEADER LOOKS EAST *In late September 1969, West Germans stunned the world by voting the Social Democrat party led by Willy Brandt, left, into power, making him the first socialist to lead a German government since 1930. Brandt came into office vowing to shake up the status quo—and to reach out to citizens in both halves of his homeland, divided since World War II into West and East Germany. In an interview in November, he told* TIME, *"It doesn't make sense to regard the other part of Germany as a foreign country like Mexico or Indonesia or even Norway. Even though it has developed into a state organization, it is still a fact that the borderline between these two parts cuts through millions of families."*

TAKING CHARGE *Muammar Gaddafi, left, the army strongman who toppled Libya's monarch King Idris in September 1969, was virtually unknown outside his country before the successful coup. Once in charge, the Arab nationalist and his nine-man junta quickly began reforming the government, curtailing special relationships with European interests that had supported the King, enforcing Islamic customs and forbidding the use of English. In December Gaddafi demanded that both the U.S. and Britain relinquish the military bases they had maintained in Libya since World War II, and they did so. Gaddafi's long, unpredictable reign had begun.*

FROM TOP: AFP—GETTY IMAGES; IMAGO—GETTY IMAGES; POPPERFOTO—GETTY IMAGES

Bernadette Devlin

In Northen Ireland, a Joan of Arc—or "Fidel Castro in a miniskirt"?

THE LONG-FESTERING WOES BETWEEN ROMAN Catholics and Protestants in predominantly Protestant Ulster, the six counties of Northern Ireland that remain loyal to the British Crown, erupted into violence early in 1969, ushering in the harrowing decades of strife called "the Troubles." They also ushered a fascinating new figure onto the world stage: 21-year-old Josephine Bernadette Devlin, who six months before had been a student at Belfast's Queen's University. Devlin had become the spokeswoman and symbol of a Catholic minority fighting the ruling Unionist Party's discrimination in jobs, housing and voting rights.

However young, Devlin was a remarkably poised and savvy political activist and a natural campaigner. On a platform, she spoke in a rapid monotone, but the words that tumbled out were impassioned and provocative; offstage, she was wholly unpretentious: "If they raise taxes, it doesn't bother me, because I don't have any money. But if they put up the price of cigarettes again, I'm done." In February she triumphed over a Unionist opponent in a by-election, and on her 22nd

birthday in April, she walked into Britain's House of Commons—straight from the Catholic barricades in Belfast—as the youngest woman ever to claim a seat.

She had come "to knock sense into [British P.M.] Harold Wilson," Devlin announced, and her voice twanged through the packed hall as she declared, "There never was born an Englishman who understands the Irish people." When she sat down, the M.P.s roared their approval. In the fall, Devlin toured the U.S., raising hundreds of thousands of dollars for her constituents from the Catholic-friendly Irish-American community.

A hero to Catholics and "Fidel Castro in a miniskirt" to Protestants, Devlin remained in Parliament until 1974. She and her husband Michael McAliskey were attacked in their home and seriously wounded by members of a Protestant guerrilla militia in 1981. Her politics have become more radical as the years have passed: since 2003, she has been denied entry to the U.S. by the State Department, a ruling that remains controversial.

Charles de Gaulle

France's giant of history steps down—and no deluge ensues

ON APRIL 29, 1969, THE CITIZENS OF FRANCE awoke to a world transformed. It hardly seemed possible, but President Charles de Gaulle was gone. At one moment he had been there, seemingly as durable as the Arc de Triomphe, the most commanding figure ruling any nation, large or small, on the face of the earth. Now, abruptly, he was a retired country gentleman of 78, a recluse in the tiny village of Colombey-les-Deux-Eglises sorting his memoirs, to be glimpsed only through a furtive telephoto lens and, most astonishing, to be heard not at all. Within 12 hours after his resignation in the wake of a referendum vote against his policies, workmen had moved his artifacts and files from the Elysée Palace. The presidential communication lines to Colombey were cut, and the other trappings of his office—except for a secretary, a bodyguard, a chauffeur and a $35,000 pension—evaporated like a morning dew. The 11-year reign of Charles de Gaulle was over; the era of Georges Pompidou had begun.

Most Frenchmen woke up in the first days of what might be called A.D. (After De Gaulle) slightly dazed and a little disbelieving at what they had wrought. Why had the hero of World War II and the founder of the Fifth Republic stepped down? The French bourgeoisie was angry and upset over France's rapid inflation and high taxes and the lingering uncertainty about the value of the franc. Big businessmen, on the other hand, were concerned about shrinking profits and the "participation" that De Gaulle had promised their workers following the chaos of the student-led riots that shut down France in the spring of 1968. The workers, in turn, resented both inflation and the higher taxes that De Gaulle had imposed in order to save the franc later in 1968. De Gaulle had juggled France's finances in an effort to satisfy both workers and businessmen; he had succeeded in pleasing neither and frightening both.

Beyond his actual deeds, his whole domineering style and omnipresent personality had become an embarrassment, or at least a source of frequent irritation. It was impossible to discuss French politics for more than a few minutes without reducing the issue to De Gaulle personally. Even the countless jokes about him had grown somewhat tiresome because they always involved the same cast: De Gaulle with God, Jesus Christ, Joan of Arc or Napoleon. Through the Gaullists'

abuse of their power over the state-owned radio and television networks, the cradle of modern revolution and free speech had become one of the free world's most tightly controlled public information centers. Politicians who opposed De Gaulle were rarely accorded air time, and pro-Gaullist propaganda assaults filled prime time during election campaigns. As for promised reforms, they came too little and too late.

Finally, the dread myth that he had created about his moment of departure had been dispelled. France simply no longer feared the "deluge" that De Gaulle so often promised would follow him. The voters had finally repaid him for his arrogance, even as they knew they would miss his grandeur. *Au revoir!*

LE GRAND CHARLES *De Gaulle attends a church service in Brittany in February 1969. He died 19 months after leaving office*

GOOD COPY *Like boxer Muhammad Ali, another star of sport's new order, Namath made his braggadocio seem appealing. Above, he charms fans and sportswriters in Miami before the game; at left, he picks apart the Colts*

Bowled Over

Underdogs Joe Namath and the Jets put the super in Super Bowl

MAYBE THEY SHOULD HAVE CALLED IT THE STUpor Bowl, considering how badly the lowly New York Jets beat up on the surprisingly hapless Baltimore Colts on Jan. 12, 1969. It was the third time that the winners of the rival National Football League and American Football League had met in a postseason match-up, but the first time since the two had merged under the National Football League umbrella. When club owners were kicking around a name for the new league's showdown, the front runner was "The Big One," until Kansas City Chiefs owner Lamar Hunt suggested "Super Bowl." So it's correct to say that the Jets won the very first contest to be called the Super Bowl, even if today we refer to the game as Super Bowl III, in what linguists call a "back formation."

Speaking of back formations, the Colts provided the pregame drama in that department. When a preseason injury put veteran quarterback Johnny Unitas on the bench, Colts coach Don Shula turned to the journey-man Earl Morrall to replace him. Morrall rose to the occasion, stunning fans by turning in his best season ever and leading the Colts into the Super Bowl on a 10-game winning streak. Unitas was ready to play by then, but Shula decided to stick with Morrall in the big game.

Jets coach Weeb Ewbank—who, deliciously, had been the Colts coach in their 1950s glory days—had no such problem: nobody was going to take away quarterback Joe Namath's job. "Broadway Joe," in fact, served double-duty for the Jets, handling their publicity needs by "guaranteeing" a victory for the Jets, listed by bookies as 18-point underdogs. But after Morrall missed the wide-open receiver Jimmy Orr on an otherwise nifty flea-flicker play at the end of the first half, the Colts ran out of steam. Shula put Unitas into the game late in the third quarter, and he led the Colts to a touchdown. Too late: the Jets won, 16-7. The day belonged to Broadway Joe, the long-haired loudmouth who dared to challenge the established order. Well, it was the '60s, after all.

"And, in the End ..."

The Beatles dream of getting back to where they once belonged

FOR THE BEATLES, THE YEAR 1969 STARTED OUT like that of millions of ordinary people around the world: they reported to work at 9 a.m. sharp on the morning of Jan. 2, ready to begin a new year and a new project. The Beatles' work, mind you, wasn't exactly ordinary. Their only goal was to create stirring music that would bring joy to legions of fans around the world. A tough job, but somebody had to do it.

But if the Beatles weren't your average working men, the project they began that morning was also utterly new to them. Rather than report to the EMI recording studios on London's Abbey Road, their longtime home base, they arrived at the vast, cold Twickenham Studio. Rather than recording late into the night, they would work film-crew hours, starting early in the morning. Rather than the very tight inner circle allowed access to their Abbey Road hideaway, they were surrounded by a full movie crew, for these sessions were to be filmed. And for three of the Beatles, there was another downer. John Lennon's inamorata, avant-garde artist Yoko Ono was present, as she had been during the sessions for 1968's *White Album*. The two had become inseparable, yet Ono found the Beatles' world utterly trivial and pointedly projected her distaste for it, a dark cloud of disapproval on the sunniest of days.

Unknown to outsiders, there were additional pressures riding on the success of the project. In a routine business meeting at the Apple offices in December 1968, Lennon told the others that he was leaving the group. A born iconoclast, he now regarded their persona as bogus and felt confined by a role he had long outgrown.

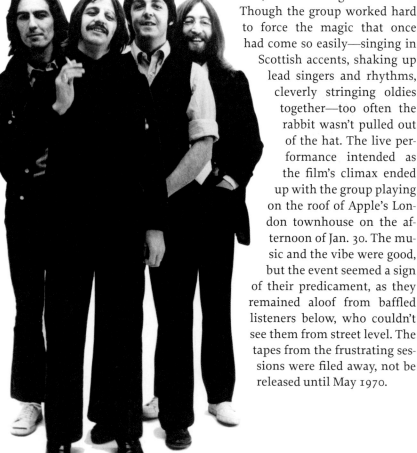

Paul McCartney, George Harrison and Ringo Starr had persuaded Lennon to stick it out for the new project, which McCartney billed as a return to the roots of the group. In fact, he already had a song to serve as the project's tent pole: *Get Back*, an upbeat invitation to "get back to where you once belonged." The concept was appealing: they would work in a stripped-down mode, eschewing the elaborately produced style of their recent records. They would cover some of the songs by older R&B artists that had influenced them. And they'd finish the project by getting back onstage, performing live for the first time since 1966. Maybe they'd stage a surprise hit-and-run show in Britain's provinces—or on an ocean liner, or, per Lennon's quip, a mental asylum.

The idea ran off the rails when it was decided that the recording sessions should be filmed: hence the unfamiliar studio, the intrusive crew, the uncongenial hours. Though the group worked hard to force the magic that once had come so easily—singing in Scottish accents, shaking up lead singers and rhythms, cleverly stringing oldies together—too often the rabbit wasn't pulled out of the hat. The live performance intended as the film's climax ended up with the group playing on the roof of Apple's London townhouse on the afternoon of Jan. 30. The music and the vibe were good, but the event seemed a sign of their predicament, as they remained aloof from baffled listeners below, who couldn't see them from street level. The tapes from the frustrating sessions were filed away, not be released until May 1970.

ΛBOVE IT ALL *The Beatles perform live for the last time, atop the Apple Records office in London, Jan. 30, 1969*

BABY, YOU'RE A RICH MAN *The Beatles pose with Lennon's Rolls-Royce; by 1969, business woes were straining their once tight bonds. At left is the iconic* Abbey Road *album cover. Paul's suit and bare feet fueled a rumor—"Paul is dead"—that had fans poring over albums for clues*

In the months that followed the demoralizing film project, John and Yoko married, as did McCartney. The last bachelor Beatle wed his American sweetheart, rock photographer Linda Eastman, on March 12. At the same time, the Beatles had to confront the failings of their Apple businesses. Though their record sales were booming, they were musicians, not businessmen. The money woes sparked more internal strife, as McCartney fought with the other three Beatles over who could best rescue the mismanaged firm.

SUMMER APPROACHED, AND WITH THE GET BACK project shelved, the group realized that they needed to release some new material. And—*presto!*—despite their recent woes, they found they had another masterpiece in them. Ironically, they summoned the muse by truly getting back to where they once belonged: recording in July and August under the masterly direction of producer George Martin, back home in the Abbey Road studios they would use for the new album's title. Even Lennon seemed delighted to be back in harness, and it showed in his powerful, swooping album opener, *Come Together,* and the blissed-out choirboy hymn *Because.* Harrison served notice that

his songwriting skills were now the equal of Lennon and McCartney's in the uplifting *ur*-Beatles tune *Here Comes the Sun* and the gorgeous ballad *Something.* TIME would later call *Something* the best song on the album, and Lennon and McCartney vocally agreed.

But the album's highlight was the stunning, sweeping suite of songs that concluded its second side, a tour de force of perfectionists McCartney and Martin. The 16-min. effort is a ravishing mosaic of song fragments that builds to a stunning climax, ending in the group's final appeal for optimism: "And in the end/ The love you take/ Is equal to the love you make." But that isn't quite the last word: after a few seconds, McCartney returns with *Her Majesty,* a cheeky mash note to the Queen that perfectly punctured any sign of pomposity.

When released in the fall, *Abbey Road* would become one of the group's greatest successes. TIME hailed it as "melodic, inventive, crammed with musical delights … the best thing the Beatles have done since *Sgt. Pepper.*" Sales were hyped after rumors spread that its cover held hints to Paul McCartney's hushed-up death. The fans' concerns were not entirely misplaced, but it was not Paul who was dead, it was the group itself. The *Abbey Road* sessions were the last time the Beatles would play together. By the spring of 1970, having failed to get themselves back to where they once belonged, the formerly Fab Four decided to finally let it be.

The Ballad of John and Yoko: Peace, Pranks and Publicity

With Bag Productions, two agile agitators explore the limits of shock art

WHEN JOHN LENNON MET YOKO ONO LATE IN 1967, the Beatles' chief rebel was living a lie: he was stranded with wife Cynthia, whom he'd married in Liverpool in 1962, and their son Julian, in a vast mansion in upscale Weybridge, often called London's "Stockbroker Belt." A fish out of water, he was miserable in this well-heeled world. After Lennon returned from the Beatles' unsatisfying visit to Maharishi Mahesh Yogi's Indian ashram, he unceremoniously dumped Cynthia for Ono, and beginning in April 1968, Lennon and Ono became inseparable.

In Ono—who, at 34 in 1968, was seven years older than he—the onetime art student Lennon found a perfect companion and muse. Like Lennon, the Japanese conceptual artist delighted in creating works that would shock, mock and distress the unhip. The pair sounded the reveille of their war on convention with the November 1968 Apple release *Two Virgins*, an experimental album perhaps crafted to annoy. Its covers featured shots of the two nude—full-frontal and, uh, full-backal—a recipe for scandal and low sales.

When the Beatles' *Get Back* sessions concluded early in 1969, John and Yoko began to link their far-out creative pursuits with their sincere crusade for world peace. Operating as Bag Productions, they created a unique mix of conceptual and performance art, rock

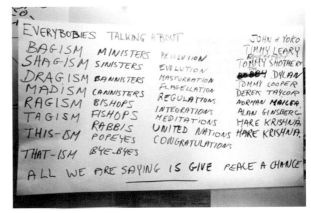

CHEAT SHEET *Lennon wrote out the nonsensical, rhyming lyrics to* Give Peace a Chance *in a laundry-list format. The last verse name-checks the participants in the makeshift recording session*

music and political protest, that is vintage 1969. On March 20, Lennon and Ono married in Gibraltar, then traveled to Amsterdam, where they holed up in a hotel suite and staged a "Bed-In for Peace," inviting the world press in to help promote their pacifist views. On their return to England, Lennon turned this offbeat odyssey into a hit Beatles single, *The Ballad of John and Yoko*. The two repeated the Bed-In in Montreal in May, where an all-star cast of non-musicians helped record *Give Peace a Chance*. The antiwar anthem resounded across the world, but many fans agreed with Beatles chronicler Philip Norman, who later decried the "heart-sinking fatuousness" of the Bed-Ins.

High on notoriety, Lennon and Ono sent acorns to world leaders, asking them to grow oak trees for peace. And on 24 hours' notice, they assembled a crew of famed musical buddies and performed as The Plastic Ono Band at a music festival in Toronto. For the holiday season, they bought billboards declaring WAR IS OVER IF YOU WANT IT. And somewhere along the way, a liberated Lennon realized that the Beatles, too, were over if you wanted it. And he did.

BED-IN CHOIR *Poet Allen Ginsberg is at far left; rock critic Paul Williams is in the right foreground. Writer Norman Mailer, not pictured, also sang on the session*

Metal Angel, Meet Jumbo Jet

Liftoff! The Concorde and Boeing 747 go wheels-up

THE BIRD THAT ROLLED OUT OF ITS HANGAR LAST week in Toulouse, France," TIME reported in March 1969, "had the ungainly look of a pterodactyl. Its drooping snout reared four stories above the tarmac; the delta wings that extended from its tubular 191-ft. body seemed barely big enough to support it. But when test pilot Andre Turcat gunned the cluster of four jet engines, the Concorde climbed swiftly and steeply. After 27 minutes of subsonic flight, it made an equally flawless, steep-pitched landing. After that, champagne corks popped around Blagnac Airport, and newspapers in Britain and France brought out big, bold headlines to celebrate." The bubbly was in order: with its maiden flight, achieved after nine costly years in development, the Concorde promised to vault Britain and France into aviation leadership as the pioneers of commercial supersonic flight. One elated European, Prince Bernhard of the Netherlands, hailed the craft as a "metal angel."

For the Concorde, such memorable moments would turn out to be disappointingly rare. Conceived in hopes of building commercial ties between France and Britain, and as a bid for leadership over the U.S. and U.S.S.R. in aviation technology, the Concorde proved a dream whose promise was always receding on the horizon. Its potential seemed enormous: the first airliner to break the sound barrier would boast a top cruising speed of 1,450 m.p.h., leaping the Atlantic in 31/2 hours. It would not only cut travel time in half; it would also beat Father Time on some flights, for passengers traveling west would arrive in New York City earlier than their departure time from London.

Yet the plane's drawbacks were apparent from its first appearance on the runway: its passenger capacity was a slim 128, while the curving sides of its narrow fuselage made its seats rather cramped; its cabin ceiling was only 6 ft. high. The roar of its quartet of engines was so intense that it was not until 1977 that the craft would be permitted to land at New York City's Kennedy Airport, and even then the plane was forbidden to achieve supersonic speed until over the Atlantic. Its limited seating capacity meant passengers had to pay a premium: by 2000, a one-way transatlantic ticket on the Concorde cost $8,148.

The supersonic ship never achieved cruising speed as a commercial airliner. Upon rollout, optimistic authorities predicted hundreds of the sleek craft would one day crisscross the globe, but in the end only 20 of them were built. When an Air France Concorde crashed upon takeoff from Paris' Charles De Gaulle Airport in 2000 after colliding with a piece of debris on the runway, killing all 109 people aboard and 4 on the ground, the Concorde was doomed; it went out of service in 2003. Today it is a museum piece: visitors to New York City's Intrepid Sea-Air-Space Museum clamber aboard to marvel at this relic of 20th century aviation dreams.

If the Concorde was a racehorse, the other great passenger ship that debuted in 1969, Boeing's enormous, humpbacked 747, proved a workhorse. Designed for maximum capacity rather than maximum speed, the 355-ton beast of burden was 231 ft. 4 in. long—threequarters the length of a football field and longer than the Wright brothers' first flight. Its 20-ft.-wide cabin was almost twice as broad as the largest passenger plane then in service, its ceilings were a roomy 8 ft. high, and it accommodated 500 passengers. In the 40 years since, Boeing has built 1,412 of the great jumbo jets, which dominate international aviation routes. Even in the skies, it seems, the tortoise beats the hare.

SPEED VS. SIZE *At top, the Concorde soars aloft, displaying its two signature attributes, swept-back delta wings and a downward-thrusting needle nose. At bottom are two views of the spacious interior of the 747, whose unique "hump" was a first-class lounge*

Ralph Nader

A crusader for consumer rights becomes the watchdog of Capitol Hill

TALK ABOUT UNEXPECTED ACCELERATION: RALPH Nader was only 32 years old in 1966, when his name first appeared in TIME's pages. Yet three years later, Nader's face was staring out from the cover of TIME's Dec. 12, 1969, issue, and the magazine described him this way: "By now, as an almost legendary crusader ... [and] the self-appointed and unpaid guardian of the interests of 204 million U.S. consumers, he has championed dozens of causes, prompted much of U.S. industry to reappraise its responsibilities and, against considerable odds, created a new climate of concern for the consumer among both politicians and businessmen. Nader's influence is greater now than ever before. That is partly because the consumer, who has suffered the steady ravishes of inflation upon his income, is less willing to tolerate substandard, unsafe or misadvertised goods."

An advocate, muckraker and crusader who trained as a lawyer, Nader by late 1969 could take credit for being almost solely responsible for the passage of six major federal laws: the National Traffic and Motor Vehicle Safety Act of 1966, the Wholesome Meat Act of 1967, the Natural Gas Pipeline Safety Act, the Radiation Control for Health and Safety Act and the Wholesale Poultry Products Act (all of 1968), and the Federal Coal Mine Health and Safety Act of 1969.

Earlier in 1969, the Ivy Leaguer of Lebanese heritage had scored a memorable victory, when General Motors stopped making its once popular Chevrolet Corvair, whose sales had plunged 93% after Nader condemned the car as a safety hazard in his 1965 best seller, *Unsafe at Any Speed.* That influential book, and Nader's later speeches, articles and congressional appearances, also forced the Department of Transportation to impose stricter safety standards on automobile and tire manufacturers.

To multiply the manpower for his campaigns, Nader had begun enlisting students on summer break, whose Zola-like zeal for investigating bureaucracies had earned them the name "Nader's Raiders." In 1968 there were only seven Raiders, but by 1969 the number had grown to 102 students, who were paid a meager living allowance to delve energetically into federal agencies in search of needed reforms.

"To many Americans," TIME said, "Nader, at 35, has become something of a folk hero, a symbol of constructive protest against the status quo ... a peaceful revolutionary ... He has never picketed, let alone occupied, a corporate office or public agency. Yet Nader has managed to cut through all the protective layers and achieve results."

CRUSADERS *Nader and his "Raiders," composed mainly of law, medical and engineering students, gather on the steps of the U.S. Capitol in 1969*

Denton Cooley
Deep in the hearts of Texas, a surgical pioneer makes history

ALTHOUGH HOUSTON'S DR. Denton A. Cooley has transplanted more human hearts than any other surgeon, he still finds them in short supply," TIME reported in its April 11, 1969, issue. "So last week he implanted the world's first completely artificial heart." The surgical breakthrough was taken as a stopgap measure while Cooley and patient Haskell Karp, 47, waited for a suitable heart donor. Karp had been linked during his transplant operation to a heart-lung machine, both breathing for him and pumping his blood, but this could keep him alive for only a few hours. Better, Cooley decided, to remove the useless heart and implant an artificial heart, leaving Karp's lungs to oxygenate his blood.

For nearly 65 hours, the artificial heart beat within Karp's chest. Then, 30 hours after the 8-oz. plastic device was replaced by the heart of a 40-year-old woman, Karp died, succumbing to pneumonia and kidney failure. His death immediately touched off an angry controversy over the wisdom of trying out the artificial device without further experimentation. It also brought into the open a feud that had long simmered between Cooley, 49, and the equally famous Dr. Michael E. DeBakey, 60, also a pioneering open-heart surgeon. The two Texans, once close colleagues, had become bitter rivals over the years. They had scrupulously avoided public battles, TIME reported in 1969, but their subordinates had been less inhibited. Those loyal to DeBakey fostered the impression that Cooley had performed some of his 20 heart transplants prematurely. Cooley's lieutenants, on the other hand, dismissed the charges as professional jealousy, pointing out that Cooley performed his first transplant three months before DeBakey did.

Cooley said that his decision to use the artificial heart, developed by Argentine-born Dr. Domingo Liotta, was made on the spur of the moment. "It was

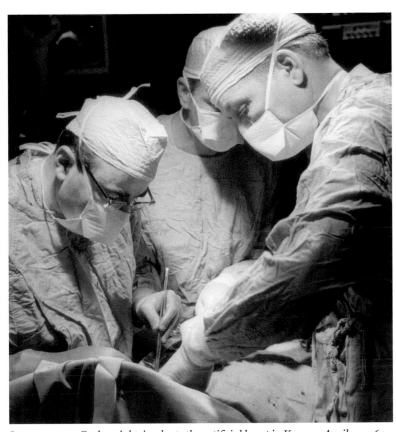

STEADY HAND *Cooley, right, implants the artificial heart in Karp on April 4, 1969*

an act of desperation," Cooley admitted. "I was concerned, of course, because this had never been done before. But we had to put up one Sputnik to start the space program, and we had to start here someplace."

Son of a Houston dentist, Cooley starred in basketball at the University of Texas, received his M.D. degree at Johns Hopkins University, studied in London with noted British heart surgeon Lord Brock, then returned to Texas to work with DeBakey at the Baylor University College of Medicine. The two men pioneered many innovations in cardiac surgery before Cooley moved to St. Luke's Episcopal Hospital, where he earned an independent reputation as a master heart surgeon and a specialist in the incredibly difficult miniaturized surgery performed on the hearts of infants. As for the two afflicted adult hearts at the center of the surgeons' long-running feud: the two men at last settled their differences in 2007, a year before DeBakey died at age 99.

Cops vs. kids *The showdown began after students and street people turned the university's vacant site into a park, above. When the school stepped in to assert control, weeks of riots ensued, including the May 20 clash at left*

Protest 101: People's Park

Kids and cops clash over a university's vacant lot in California

LIKE THE 1960S THEMSELVES, PEOPLE'S PARK IN BERkeley, Calif., started out well enough but soon got way out of hand. The troubles began with a dusty, three-acre tract of land owned by the University of California, Berkeley, in a dowdy neighborhood near the campus. Planned as a park for university folk, it had become a vacant eyesore after funds ran short. In April 1969, Berkeley students and local "street people"—a motley crew of hippies and vagrants—took over the plot. They plowed the ground and, with $1,000 raised among themselves and neighborhood businessmen, planted trees, flowers and grass and installed benches, a sandbox and swings. Up went a sign: PEOPLE'S PARK.

Then, as TIME reported, "With all the thoughtfulness of laboratory animals responding to electric stimulation, the university reacted." On May 15, Chancellor Roger Heyns and the city took action. In came 300 policemen and bulldozers, up went an 8-ft. fence, and out went about 75 street people. Lift-off! In a few hours,

some 1,800 Berkeley students marched to the site and began battling with cops, hurling rocks and taunts. Police responded with tear gas and 12-gauge shotguns firing low-velocity birdshot. Street person James Rector, 25, was killed; another protester was blinded.

After a 3-hr. skirmish, about 60 people had been sent to the hospital (including 20 police), 36 protesters were under arrest, and one car had been burned. When striking students began staging daily protests that rocked the campus, Governor Ronald Reagan sent National Guard troops to restore order. Result: a tear-gas assault at the school—and more protest marches that bred new clashes between cops and kids, resulting in 150 injuries on both sides and nearly 900 arrests.

Flash-forward 40 years: today, the site is a public park maintained by the university and community groups working together—great idea! But is it a sweet oasis of green or a crime-infested magnet for derelicts? As in the '60s, the answer you get depends on the person you ask.

Burn On, Big River

When a Cleveland waterway catches fire and an oil spill fouls the California coast, Americans awaken to the planet's woes

SOME RIVER!" *TIME* SNEERED, IN AN UNUSUAL FIT of derision in its Aug. 1, 1969, issue. "Chocolate-brown, oily, bubbling with subsurface gases, it oozes rather than flows." The target of the magazine's scorn: Cleveland's Cuyahoga River, which had provoked both repulsion and grim jests around the nation when its oil-slicked waters burst into flames on June 22, burning with such intensity that two railroad bridges spanning it were nearly destroyed.

The magazine summoned three witnesses to testify to the sorry state of the waterway on which the great city was founded. First it quoted government experts from the Federal Water Pollution Control Administration, whose recent study of the river concluded, "The lower Cuyahoga has no visible life, not even low forms such as leeches and sludge worms that usually thrive on wastes." Next up: Cleveland's mayor, Carl Stokes, who lamented to the magazine, "What a terrible reflection on our city." The last word belonged to the citizens of Cleveland, whose frequent jest *TIME* printed, "People who fall into the Cuyahoga don't drown. They decay."

Cleveland was not alone in its misery in 1969. On the West Coast, the pristine white-sand beaches of wealthy Santa Barbara, north of Los Angeles, were fouled early in the year by an 800-sq.-mi.-wide oil slick, formed when petroleum seeped from busted pipes on an aging Union Oil drilling platform off the coast. "Wherever it shifted," *TIME* reported in its Feb. 21 issue, "the oil brought ecological disaster to bird and sea life. At Santa Barbara's three treatment centers, 1,400 sea-diving birds had been brought in. Only a third survived. Other shoreline birds, such as curlews, plovers and willets,

which feed on sand creatures, had fled the area … The bodies of six seals floated onto Santa Barbara beaches. Autopsies performed on one of three dead dolphins showed that its blowhole had been clogged with oil, causing massive lung hemorrhages."

The 1960s are often portrayed as a period of utopian dreams and revolutionary schemes, all of which failed to materialize. But among the lasting legacies of the period's social activism is our modern understanding of the importance of the environment, which was sparked in part by the woes of 1969—even if the sparks emerged from a polluted, burning river. Yes, the Cuyahoga fire produced black humor along the lines of songwriter Randy Newman's hilarious tune *Burn On* ("Cleveland, city of light, city of magic … 'Cause the Cuyahoga River/Goes smokin' through my dreams"). But it also led to a widespread public outcry for action, which bred lasting, significant results.

By late October 1969, *TIME* was reporting on "a new conservationist passion: using the law as a weapon to help save the environment … the nation's rising awareness of ecology has moved scores of judges to listen." The Federal Government was also roused to action: on Dec. 2, 1970, the Environmental Protection Agency, proposed by President Richard Nixon, began operation. In 1977 the federal Clean Water Act was passed by Congress. But this was everyone's problem: in 1969, environmental activists began proposing an annual "Earth Day," in which ordinary citizens would pause to honor the planet and work toward its sustainable future. Heeding the call, Americans celebrated the first Earth Day on April 22, 1970. Burn on, big river.

ENVIRONMENT IN PERIL *At top, authorities monitor water quality in Ohio's Cuyahoga River in 1968, along a stretch that was being used as an automobile junkyard. Below, California state conservation crews clean up oil-soaked straw in Santa Barbara*

RESPONSE *On July 27, 1969, a month after the Stonewall ruckus, protesters assembled for New York City's first Gay Pride March*

EYEWITNESS

Stonewall—and Other Walls

Writer Edmund White recalls a defining moment for gays

In the early-morning hours of June 28, 1969, New York City police raided the Stonewall Inn, a Greenwich Village bar frequented by gays. But many patrons fought back, and in the weeks that followed, gays began to organize and march to demand an end to official harassment. The events, little noticed at the time outside Manhattan, are now considered a watershed moment for the gay-rights movement. Writer Edmund White, whose memoirs A Boy's Own Story *(1982) and* The Beautiful Room Is Empty *(1988) chronicle his life as a young gay man at the time, was present that night, and he shared these recollections with* TIME *in 2009.*

ON THE NIGHT OF THE RIOT, I WAS WALKING TO MY apartment in the Village with a friend of mine, around 1 in the morning. We weren't in the bar; we were just walking past it. And we saw a crowd of people standing in front of it, who were very angry. People were backed up against the fence of the park all the way across the street and the area was so crowded that cars couldn't go through. The police were arresting people and throwing them into a Black Maria van.

My first reaction was a totally middle-class one: "Calm down guys. Come on, let's not do this; let's not get into trouble." But two very good organizers happened to be there: one was Jim Fouratt, who had led a Be-In, a hippie/Flower Child event in Central Park. The other was Craig Rodwell, who then owned the Oscar Wilde Memorial Bookshop on Christopher Street in the Village, which just closed in 2009. Craig was a real, unapologetic militant. They rallied the crowd and kept people from retreating.

In some ways, it was an absurd scene. Gay men would dash down the street and confront a phalanx of police by kicking up like a chorus line. Within 20 minutes, I got excited and carried away. Suddenly, for a moment, I felt a flicker of anger and collective identity—I had never felt that way before.

The first Black Maria had pulled away, and the police who were left behind were starting to get frightened, so they retreated inside the bar with a bunch of people they had arrested, and barricaded the door. Then somebody ripped a parking meter out of the sidewalk and used it as a battering ram to break down the door. Soon, people were lighting garbage cans and throwing them through the windows. We wanted to free the prisoners inside.

Suddenly, middle-class white gays who were very used to being captured in raids on men's rooms were fighting back against the police. You can't imagine how empowering this was for a group who had listened for years to stories about married men who had been arrested and publicly humiliated—and then committed suicide.

The stand-off lasted for hours, and the police never managed to chase us away. It finally ended when the sun started to come up, and everybody was tired. But we never retreated. So I went home with my friend. The next morning, we read the New York *Times* to find the coverage … and there was nothing. I guess at the time this story defined the kind of news that wasn't "fit to print."

Even so, this, for us, was the first time that gay men hadn't picked up their skirts and run away. Stonewall instantly became the gay equivalent of storming the Bastille, a fantastic symbol. A group of us started calling ourselves the Pink Panthers. The whole idea of a gay movement struck us as funny, almost ridiculous—both amusing and legitimizing at the same time. I remember writing the next day: "This may be the first funny revolution."

In those days, we gay people didn't think of ourselves as a minority group. We thought of ourselves as having a sickness. After all, homosexuality was officially considered a psychological disease by the U.S. medical establishment. All of us, including me, wanted to go straight. My friends were going to straight shrinks and getting engaged to girls and ruining their lives. There was always a ritual moment at the end of every evening when we'd look at each other and say, "God, we're sick!" I had a boyfriend who was given electroshock and hospitalized.

At Stonewall, a spark leapt from the wider culture of liberation that was happening all around us, and fired up our isolated world. Thanks to the rhetoric and reality of liberation for blacks and other oppressed groups, along with the antiwar movement, people suddenly put all these things together. "Black is beautiful" led directly to one of the slogans shouted outside Stonewall that night: "Gay is good!" After Stonewall, gays became much more visible—to one another, if not to the outside world. At Stonewall, we first began to form a community and an ideology.

The Spirit of 1969

Sex, drugs and rock 'n' roll defined the year—like it or not!

AMERICANS WERE SMACK IN THE MIDDLE OF A SEXUAL REVOLUTION IN 1969, AND *TIME* addressed the subject in a cover story that featured Adam and Eve wearing fig leaves. "An erotic renaissance (or rot, as some would have it) is upon the land," said the magazine. "Owing to a growing climate of permissiveness—and the Pill—Americans today have more sexual freedom than any previous generation … What seems truly startling is not so much what Americans do but what they may see, hear and read … From stage and screen, printed page and folk-rock jukeboxes, society is bombarded with coital themes. Writers bandy four-letter words as if they had just completed a deep-immersion Berlitz course in Anglo-Saxon."

FOUR'S A CROWD *Among the entries in the mainstream media's newfound obsession with sexuality: Paul Mazursky's film* Bob & Carol & Ted & Alice *(starring, from left, Elliott Gould, Natalie Wood, Robert Culp, Dyan Cannon), an attempt to turn wife-swapping into a mainstream comedy.* TIME's *verdict: "These swimming-pool Swifts smugly mock a situation that they simultaneously exploit … [the movie] suggests that sex is too important to be left to Hollywood." Words that ring true, 40 years on.*

SHOW OF SUPPORT *The liberation of women from their subordinate role as the "second sex" was one of the most significant social changes ushered in by the 1960s. The movement began in the early '60s (Betty Friedan's* The Feminine Mystique *appeared in 1963) but languished during the chaotic years that followed. Even in 1969, attempts to redefine women's roles often seemed a sort of novelty rather than a serious issue. Above, a largely male crowd gathers to watch a woman doff her bra in a demonstration outside a San Francisco department store. In a more realistic, if less sensational, protest over dress codes, many women employees of CBS wore slacks to work on the same day in 1969, in protest against a management order forbidding them.*

BROADWAY GOES BARE *Perfectly timing the public mood, British theater critic and dramaturge Kenneth Tynan's* Oh! Calcutta! *brought the sexual revolution to the mainstream stage. The show strung together a series of brief scenes and dances, most of them featuring naked or nearly naked actors, that dissected, lampooned and celebrated human sexuality. Several well-known artists contributed short efforts to the revue, including Samuel Beckett, Jules Feiffer and John Lennon. Most critics hated the revue, more for its scanty entertainment value than its scanty costume budget. But* TIME's *T.E. Kalem was surprisingly kind: "A dance of love [left] has the silvery sensuousness of a pas de deux performed under the moon," he wrote, "and Director Jacques Levy elicits cast responses that are fluid, intimate, and disciplined."*

DARE TO BARE *The miniskirt, introduced in the mid-'60s, remained the rage in 1969, as exemplified by the young model above. Fashion designers, however, went to great lengths in introducing their choice for the Next Big Thing, the maxi-skirt. At top right is a zebra-stripe maxi-coat from London designer Michael of Carlos Place; the model's Afro-style hat and the coat's animal-skin motif reflect the impact of African-American style, as seen in the snazzy, leopard-skin men's outfit at top left. Meanwhile, hippies stuck to their perennial styles: long skirts, lots of layers, floral and Indian prints, buckskin fringe and facial hair for men. Revealing styles were popular, with women favoring brief tops that showed off the midriff, as in the Manhattan street shot at bottom right.*

MOUTH OF THE SOUTH *She was the talk of Washington in 1969—and she did most of the talking. TIME called Martha Mitchell, wife of Attorney General John Mitchell, "the warbler of Watergate" (the apartment complex, not the later scandal). The Pine Bluff, Ark., native shared her views with TIME, "Any time you get somebody marching in the streets, it's catering to revolution. It started with the colored people in the South. Now other groups are taking to the streets."*

LOFTY AMBITIONS *Mercury 7 Astronaut John Glenn, who made history (and the cover of TIME) in 1962 by becoming the first American to orbit the planet, declared in December 1969 that he would run for the Senate seat in his*

native Ohio vacated by retiring Democrat Stephen Young in 1970.

Glenn first attempted to take Young's seat in 1964. But that bid ended in frustration and dizzy spells when he took a header on a bath mat, injured his inner ear and had to pull out of the race. "It will be the dirtiest campaign ever," Glenn promised. "I won't take a bath."

UNDONE *"I'm interested in anything about revolt, disorder, chaos, especially activity that has no meaning. It seems to me to be the road to freedom," front man Jim Morrison of the L.A. rock group the Doors told TIME in 1967, when he was only 23. The UCLA graduate and son of a U.S. Navy admiral also told the magazine, "We hide ourselves in the music to reveal ourselves."*

Two years later, it was Morrison's alleged failure to restrict his revelations to his music that led to the biggest crisis of his career. Days after he gave a drunken, rambling performance at a March 1 Doors concert in Miami, Dade County police issued a warrant for his arrest for allegedly exposing himself during the show. The charges were never proved, and Morrison has been exonerated over time, but in the short run the incident caused the Doors to cancel valuable concert bookings and forced Morrison into a long legal nightmare. He would die in Paris only two years later, in July 1971.

CAT FIGHT! *Oh, that Truman Capote. The pint-sized writer had an oversized opinion of his gifts, a dim view of many of his fellow writers and a tongue that frequently outpaced his inner censor—a recipe for delicious scandal. Early in 1969, Capote described novelist Jacqueline Susann, author of the steamy '60s best sellers* The Love Machine *and* Valley of the Dolls, *as resembling "a truck driver in drag." When Susann turned up on Johnny Carson's* Tonight Show *in September, millions of Americans stayed up late, awaiting her response—but the subject never came up.*

Not to worry; Carson was waiting to pounce. Just as the writer was about to leave, her host asked innocently, "What do you think of Truman?" "Truman … Truman," she pondered. "I think history will prove he was one of the best Presidents we've had."

THE ONCE-OVER *While President Nixon greets Joan Kennedy, wife of Massachusetts Senator Edward M. Kennedy, at a March 12 White House reception for members of Congress, Pat Nixon appears to be performing some rapid calculations as to the length of Mrs. Kennedy's hemline. She was not alone: most women guests at the function followed the First Lady's lead and wore floor-length gowns.*

SALAD DAYS *She had only recently been divorced from Frank Sinatra, and he was between two career-defining roles—Benjamin Braddock in* The Graduate *and Ratso Rizzo in* Midnight Cowboy—*when* TIME *put Mia Farrow, 23, and Dustin Hoffman, 31, on the cover of its Feb. 7, 1969, issue, just before their long-forgotten film* John and Mary *opened. In their lack of traditional star power,* TIME *found the signs of a new authenticity in American film. "There have been haunted girls and unprepossessing men before—Audrey Hepburn was never known for her measurements, and Humphrey Bogart commanded affection even though he looked accident-prone. But there has never before been such a crowd of real faces, so many young actors resembling young audiences— and young audiences pay for 65% of the movie tickets in America."*

CLOCKWISE FROM TOP: AP IMAGES, BETTMANN CORBIS, JOHN DOMINIS—TIME LIFE PICTURES

A man went looking for America.
And couldn't find it anywhere...

Cannes Film
Festival
WINNER
"Best Film
By a New
Director"

PANDO COMPANY in association with
RAYBERT PRODUCTIONS presents **easy RiDeR**
starring
PETER FONDA · DENNIS HOPPER · JACK NICHOLSON

Written by   Directed by   Produced by   Associate Producer   Executive Producer
PETER FONDA   DENNIS HOPPER   PETER FONDA   WILLIAM HAYWARD   BERT SCHNEIDER · COLOR
DENNIS HOPPER   Released by COLUMBIA PICTURES
TERRY SOUTHERN

Western Visions

Saddle up! In 1969 the movies explored cowboys of all
stripes, from John Wayne to Jon Voight, from rebels on
chrome steeds to Butch Cassidy and the Sundance Kid

F ROM HUCK FINN AND THE RUNAWAY SLAVE JIM ON A RAFT TO ISHMAEL AND QUEEQUEG ON
the *Pequod* to Kirk and Spock on the *Enterprise*, it's one of the great recurring themes of
American culture: two buddies unite to light out for the territories, in search of freedom
and adventure—or maybe just to escape society's dead hand. The westering theme can be
expressed in hundreds of variations, and the most interesting movies of 1969 provide a fascinating
glimpse of its possibilities. Two classic Westerns stuck to familiar ground: in *True Grit*, veteran
John Wayne, as crusty lawman Rooster J. Cogburn, paired up with a most unlikely buddy, a
young girl seeking to avenge her father's death. Justice was served, both in the movie and at the
Academy Awards, where Wayne finally won a long overdue Oscar for Best Actor. In *Butch Cassidy
and the Sundance Kid*, director George Roy Hill updated the Western genre for modern audiences.
His pair of desperadoes, played by Paul Newman and Robert Redford, put fresh new faces on a
well-worn format, and moviegoers loved the playful knowingness of the film and its stars.

Two other memorable "Westerns" stretched the theme in surprising directions. In the daring
Midnight Cowboy, set in Manhattan, Jon Voight played a male hustler from Texas seeking to escape
his world, while Dustin Hoffman played his derelict sidekick. And in *Easy Rider*, Hollywood
rebels Peter Fonda and Dennis Hopper created a '60s Western, replacing horses with motorcycles
and using psychedelic drugs to explore the frontiers of consciousness rather than geography.

EASY RIDER *Like the era it captured so well, this '69 hit was (and is) a mess. "It is unwatchable—unless you are benefiting from the illegal substances it advocates," said critic David Thomson in his 2008 book* Have You Seen? *Among its sins: poor cinematography and a confusing plot. Yet it is also a landmark in U.S. cinema: shot on a shoestring by Hollyood rebels Dennis Hopper and Peter Fonda, who took the lead roles of Billy and Captain America, the film perfectly captured the late-'60s zeitgeist, in which society is a monster and only those who defy its laws are pure of heart. "The film has refurbished the classic romantic gospel of the outcast wanderer," said* TIME's *1969 review.*

Easy Rider's huge success ushered in the most creative era of Hollywood's history: TIME *later called it "the little film that killed the big picture." It also introduced a new star in Jack Nicholson, playing a small-town lawyer who is martyred for befriending the rebels. Above: Hopper, Fonda and Nicholson; at right, the trippy trio and friends on the road in Cannes.*

BUTCH CASSIDY AND THE
SUNDANCE KID *At a time when
the western picture seemed ready to
ride into the sunset, director George
Roy Hill brought the genre roaring
back to life with a newfangled take
that charmed audiences then and
remains a beloved classic now.
The secret: pick stars glittering
with charisma (veteran Paul
Newman and handsome newcomer
Robert Redford), then fit them out
with 1960s attitudes and 1890s
getups. If at times the results seem
as profoundly inauthentic as a
cowpoke warbling a Burt Bachrach/
Hal David song—well, welcome to
Hollywood. The top-grossing film
of 1969 won four Oscar Awards.
Above, Redford and Newman; at
right, the studly stars horse around
with director Hill on location in
Mexico in 1968.*

MIDNIGHT COWBOY *Director John Schlesinger's tale of a male hustler (Jon Voight) and the ailing derelict he befriends (Dustin Hoffman) was "one of the least likely and most melancholy love stories in the history of the American film," said* TIME'S *1969 review. As Joe Buck, "a strutting phallus … who swings from both sides of the bed," Voight trolled lower Manhattan looking "as out of place as a stallion in a parking lot." Hoffman, who had vaulted to stardom in 1968 in* The Graduate, *was unforgettable as the dying Ratso Rizzo. Buoyed by folksinger Fred Neil's haunting song* Everybody's Talkin', *the film was a major success, though its sex scenes were highly provocative at the time. Despite its X rating, it won Oscars for Best Picture and Best Director.*

THEY SHOOT HORSES, DON'T THEY? *Director Sydney Pollack's dark journey into an America laid waste by the 1930s Depression began a career revival for star Jane Fonda, who went on to win a Best Actress Oscar for* Klute, *released in 1971.*

Also starring Michael Sarrazin (left, with Fonda), Red Buttons and Gig Young, the forceful melodrama of plucky kids who endure the horrors of a dance marathon for money was a major hit and was nominated for nine Oscars. However, TIME *found the actors were better than Pollack's overwrought direction: "The music goes round and round, and so do the actors, in a coruscating dance of death. It is a pity that the picture is not left to them. The filmmakers should have known better than to cling to undimensional symbolism and stylistic conceits. They shoot movies, don't they?"*

THE LOVE BUG *It will never be mistaken for another* Midnight Cowboy *or* Easy Rider, *but the Walt Disney comedy about a likable Volkswagen bug named Herbie was a charming movie for kids that has proved almost as durable as the '68 Beetle of the title. After a limited release in the last week of 1968, it went on to become one of the highest-grossing films of 1969. True to the Disney formula, the hit spawned a clutch of successful follow-ups. The franchise was most recently dusted off and sprayed with new-car scent in 2005, when* Herbie Fully Loaded *starred Disney remake queen Lindsay Lohan. At right are original stars Buddy Hackett, Benson Fong, Michele Lee, Dean Jones and, uh, Herbie.*

TRUE GRIT *When* TIME *put veteran star John Wayne on its cover in 1969 for his role as a crusty sheriff in Henry Hathaway's charming western yarn, it noted, "The public has watched the celluloid Wayne pass through three stages of life. In the '30s, he was the outspoken, hair-trigger-tempered son who would straighten out if he didn't get shot first. By the late '40s, he had graduated to fatherhood: topkick Marine to a platoon of shavetails or trail boss to a bunch of saddle tramps. In* True Grit *his belt disappears into his abdomen, his opinions are sclerotic, and his face is beginning to crack like granite." Fans welcomed the 62-year-old's concession to reality, making* True Grit *a late-career exclamation point for Wayne, whose turn as the disheveled, drunken Reuben J. "Rooster" Cogburn—a portrait in growing old disgracefully— brought him an overdue Oscar for Best Actor.*

Out of Control

A young woman's tragic death and a Senator's failure to act

F ORTY YEARS LATER, THE QUESTION PEOPLE ASKED IN the immediate wake of the tragedy that blotted the character and career of Massachusetts Senator Edward M. Kennedy remains germane: What was he thinking? Here are the facts of the case, as TIME first reported them: "Kennedy's career was threatened not by a violent enemy or a political foe but by a scandal that revealed a shocking lapse of judgment and control. Kennedy's lost night on Chappaquiddick [Island] off Martha's Vineyard and the mystifying week that followed brought back all the old doubts [about his character]. For approximately nine hours after the car that he was driving plunged from Dike Bridge [into Poucha Pond]—carrying his only passenger, Mary Jo Kopechne, [a 28-year-old aide in Kennedy-family political campaigns], to a death by drowning—Kennedy failed to notify police. After his first brief and inadequate statement at the station house, his silence allowed time for both honest questions and scurrilous gossip to swirl around his reputation and his future."

Days after the July 18 accident, Kennedy, who had become the torchbearer of his family's political ambitions after the assassinations of his two older brothers, withdrew his initial opposition to misdemeanor proceedings against him and pleaded guilty to a charge of leaving the scene of an accident. That night, on national TV, he told his version of the events, assuming full responsibility for his failure to report the incident. "I was overcome," the Senator said, by "grief, fear, doubt, exhaustion, panic, confusion and shock." He was never punished by the courts for his deed—but the scandal put his presidential aspirations on hold until 1980, when he failed to displace incumbent Jimmy Carter on the Democratic ticket. Kopechne's family is reported to have received an undisclosed sum of money as a settlement from the Senator's family.

As for Kennedy, he put his nose to the grindstone in the Senate, where over the decades, he has distinguished himself. Though his liberal stands still draw the wrath of political foes, when the Senator received a diagnosis of brain cancer in 2008, the expressions of concern that arose from both sides of the Senate and from a broad swath of Americans showed that the story of Chappaquiddick is not simply a tale of indiscretion, irresponsibility and a young life tragically lost but also a story of ultimate redemption.

overturned car but wa
of Washington,D.C.,who
etary for the late Se

BETTMANN CORBIS

AFTERMATH *A contemporary file photo shows Senator Kennedy's*

1967 Oldsmobile being hauled out of Poucha Pond on Chappaquiddick Island. Earlier, Mary Jo Kopechne's body was found in the back seat

"The *Eagle* Has Landed"

Meeting a historic challenge, the U.S. puts two men on the moon

WHAT DOES HISTORY LOOK LIKE? FOR MILLIONS of people around the world who watched one of the most momentous events in the long story of human progress at the moment it took place, history looked like two small, bright objects moving around in strangely weightless fashion against a gloomy, dark backdrop, as seen on flickering, smallish TV screens. The date was July 20, 1969, and two Americans had just backed their way down a ladder and become the first men to stand on the surface of the moon.

When the first astronaut, Neil Armstrong, reached the surface, he began moving about in the harsh light of the lunar morning with a cautious, almost shuffling gait. "The surface is fine and powdery; it adheres in fine layers, like powdered charcoal, to the soles and sides of my foot," he said. "I can see the footprints of my boots and the treads in the fine, sandy particles." Minutes later, Armstrong was joined by Edwin (Buzz) Aldrin.

Then, gaining confidence with every step, the two jumped and loped across the barren landscape for 2 hr. 14 min., enjoying their buoyancy in the moon's light gravitational field, while the TV camera they had set up some 50 ft. from the landing module, *Eagle*, transmitted their movements to the enthralled viewers on Earth, a quarter of a million miles away. Sometimes moving in surrealistic slow motion, sometimes bounding around like exuberant kangaroos, they set up experiments and scooped up rocks, snapped pictures and probed the soil, apparently enjoying every moment of their stay in the moon's alien environment.

After centuries of dreams and prophecies, the moment had come. Mankind had broken its terrestrial shackles for the first time and set foot on another world. Standing on the lifeless, rock-studded surface, the two Apollo 11 astronauts could see Earth, a lovely blue and white hemisphere suspended in the velvety

A LONG SALUTE *While Aldrin stands on the moon, wife Joan and friends give a resounding cheer, some 240,000 miles away*

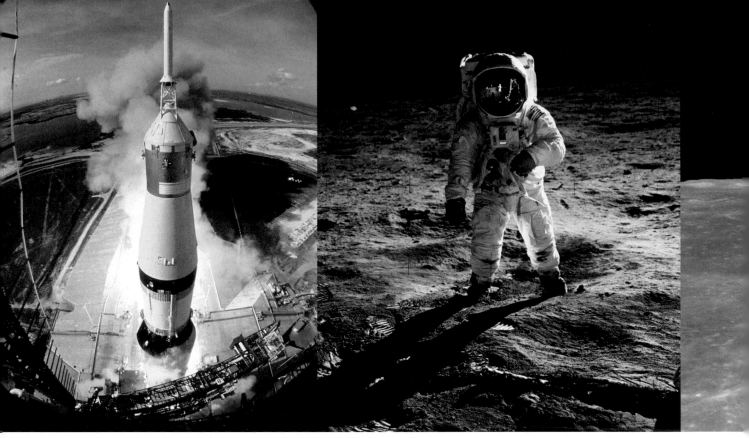

TIMELINE *Above, from left, the Saturn V rocket blasts off on July 16, and Aldrin stands on the moon's surface. At right, the lunar*

black sky. Although the two men planted an American flag on the moon, their feat was far more than an occasion for national pride. It was a stunning scientific and intellectual accomplishment for a creature that, in the space of a few million years—an instant in evolutionary chronology—emerged from primeval forests to hurl himself at the stars.

THE HISTORIC FIRST STEPS ON THE MOON WERE taken four days after a giant Saturn V rocket—at 6,484,289 lbs. the heaviest space vehicle ever launched—fired its jets, shook loose some 1,000 Ibs. of ice that had frozen on its white sides and roared aloft. Its passage to the moon helped build suspense for the long-awaited highlight of the mission: *Eagle's* undocking from *Columbia,* the command module, and its descent to the moon. No work of the imagination, however contrived, could have rivaled it for excitement, suspense and, finally, triumph.

When the orbiting command module and the lunar module (LM) emerged from behind the moon, having undocked while they were out of radio communication, Armstrong boasted, "The Eagle has wings." The lunar module, with Armstrong and Aldrin aboard, was ready for its landing on the moon, while Michael Collins remained aboard *Columbia*—a supporting role the popular astronaut accepted with typical good grace.

Behind the moon again, on their 14th revolution, *Eagle's* descent engine was fired, slowing the lander down and dropping it into an orbit that would take it to within 50,000 ft. of the lunar surface. Moments later the engine fired again, a 12-min. burn that was scheduled to end only when the craft was within two yards of the surface. One of the most dangerous parts of Apollo 11's long journey had begun.

Now the tension was obvious in the voices of both the crew and the controller. Just 160 ft. from the surface, Aldrin reported, "Quantity light." That signaled that only 114 sec. of fuel remained. Armstrong and Aldrin had 40 sec. to decide if they could land within the next 20 sec. If they could not, they would have to abort, jettisoning their descent stage and firing their ascent engine to return to *Columbia.* At that critical point, *Eagle's* computer reported, "Program alarm." The relatively primitive machine was being asked to make too many calculations in the frenetic moments before touchdown. It had begun to balk at having to track *Columbia* while also making the final descent.

Mission Control quickly spotted the cause and ordered the rendezvous radar turned off to remedy the situation. And then, unhappy with the terrain of the landing site, Armstrong, a 39-year-old civilian with 23 years of experience at flying everything from Ford Trimotors to experimental X-15 rocket planes, took over

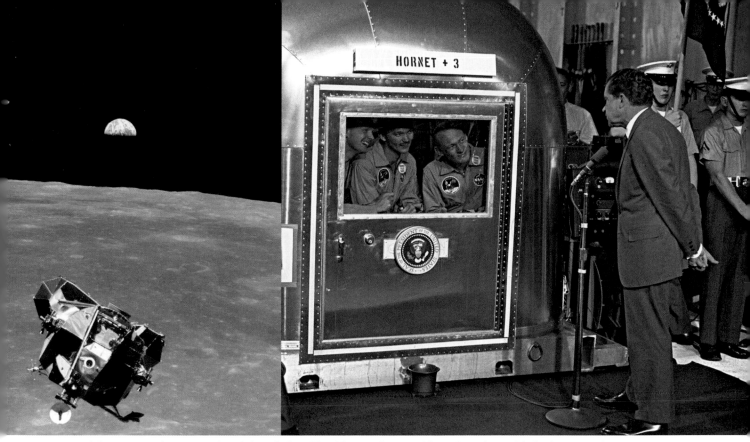

module returns to the command module to dock and head home, where President Nixon chats with the decompressing crew

the manual controls. Had he not done so, the LM might have set down in an area strewn with boulders; the crisis emphasized the value of manned flight.

Then came the word that the world had been waiting for. "Houston," Armstrong called. "Tranquillity Base here. The *Eagle* has landed." The time: 4:17:41 p.m., E.T., only a few minutes earlier than the landing time scheduled months before. It was a wild, incredible moment. There were cheers, tears and frantic applause at Mission Control in Houston, which told the crew, "There's lots of smiling faces in this room, and all over the world." "There are two of them up here," responded *Eagle.* "And don't forget the one up here," Collins piped in from the orbiting *Columbia.*

FOR THE NEXT THREE HOURS, ARMSTRONG AND Aldrin made all *Eagle* systems ready for a quick takeoff should that become necessary. Then, eager to explore their new world, they were given permission to skip their scheduled sleep period and walk on the surface some four hours earlier than planned.

Armstrong and Aldrin struggled to put on their boots, gloves, helmets and backpacks. On his way down the stairway, Armstrong pulled a lanyard and exposed the miniature camera that televised the remainder of his historic descent. Because the camera had to be stowed upside down, for a few seconds, Armstrong was turned

topsy-turvy in the picture; a NASA television converter quickly righted the image.

Once on the moon, even the taciturn Armstrong could not contain himself. Back home, as his wife Janet watched on TV, she urged, "Be descriptive now, Neil." Yet suddenly he began to bubble over with detailed descriptions and to snap pictures with all the enthusiasm of the archetypal tourist. Houston had to remind him four times to quit clicking and move to his assigned task: gathering "contingency" samples of lunar soil that would guarantee the return of at least some material if the mission had to be suddenly aborted. "Just as soon as we finish these pictures," said Armstrong.

Only seconds after Aldrin touched the surface, he jumped back up to the first rung of the ladder three times to show how easy it was. Then, delighted with his new-found agility despite the 183 Ibs. of clothing and gear that he carried, he became the first man to break into a run on the lunar surface.

During the next two hours, the astronauts planted a 3-ft. by 5-ft. American flag, stiffened with thin wire so that it would appear to be waving in the vacuum of the moon. They set up three scientific devices: one to measure solar wind, another to record moonquakes and meteor impacts, a third for precisely measuring Earth-moon distances. Aldrin, assigned to collect core samples, was to have dug some 13 in. into the moon's

LUNAR LEGENDS *The Apollo 11 crew poses for posterity with their target as a backdrop. From left, Neil Armstrong, Michael Collins and Buzz Aldrin*

surface, but after hammering the tool vigorously, he drove it no more than 9 in. deep. Moments later, the men stopped to receive a congratulatory phone message from President Richard Nixon.

Two hours and 31 minutes after Armstrong first emerged, both men climbed back inside *Eagle*. In addition to the flag, the astronauts left behind a number of mementoes from Earth, including a small silicon disk bearing statements (reduced in size 200 times) by Presidents Eisenhower, Kennedy, Johnson and Nixon, as well as words of goodwill from leaders of 72 different countries and Pope Paul VI. Attached to a leg of the lunar module's lower stage, which would remain on the moon when the upper portion blasted off, was a plaque signed by President Nixon and the astronauts. It read: HERE MEN FROM THE PLANET EARTH FIRST SET FOOT UPON THE MOON, JULY 1969 A.D. WE CAME IN PEACE FOR ALL MANKIND.

Some 21 hours after landing on the moon, Armstrong and Aldrin blasted off in the five-ton upper stage of the lunar module, then rendezvoused and docked with the orbiting *Columbia* and set off for the long voyage back to a planet transfixed by their deeds.

ACROSS THE GULF OF SPACE, *TIME* REPORTED, EARTHlings had followed the epic journey of Apollo 11 with fascination. In Paris, backup electrical generators were turned on to keep TV tubes glowing through the night. Czechoslovakia issued commemorative stamps; Poles unveiled a soaring statue at the

Krakow sports stadium in honor of the astronauts. Newspapers the world over strove to outdo one another, breaking out what pressmen call "Second Coming" type. Almost alone in the world, the mainland Chinese press virtually ignored the moon landing, though one Maoist Hong Kong daily headlined, THE AMERICAN PEOPLE PRAY: GOD GIVE ME A PIECE OF BREAD, DON'T GIVE ME THE MOON.

Americans, so often divided in 1969, united to cheer the triumph, recalling that when John F. Kennedy committed the U.S. to landing men on the moon before the end of the 1960s, virtually none of the equipment capable of making the half-million-mile journey existed. Now, eight years later, a great spaceship made of more than 15 million parts redeemed Kennedy's pledge with five months to spare—a remarkable accomplishment, and all the more remarkable for the fact that man did not actually enter the space age until 1957, when the Soviet Union launched Sputnik.

Before Kennedy issued his lunar challenge, the nation's entire manned space experience totaled 15 min. 20 sec.—the length of Alan Shepard's suborbital fling down the Atlantic test range on May 5, 1961. Rockets had been blowing up on their Cape Canaveral launch pads with humiliating frequency; from 1958 to 1964, the U.S. suffered 13 straight failures in its efforts to send rockets around or onto the moon. Now, thanks to the biggest and most imaginative government-industry-university team ever put together for a single project, the challenge had been met. At its peak in 1966, Apollo involved 400,000 men and women at 120 universities and laboratories and 20,000 industrial firms.

Four days later, aboard the U.S.S. *Hornet*, 950 miles southwest of Hawaii, hundreds of crewmen, reporters, cameramen and VIP guests eagerly scanned the predawn skies. At 5:41 a.m., shouts of "There it is! There it is!" rose from the aircraft carrier's huge flight deck. For a split second, a tiny orange speck, no brighter than a faint shooting star, shone against the thick, purplish clouds. Apollo 11 had come home, splashing down in the Pacific to a heroes' welcome.

The astronauts' journey concluded as flawlessly as it had begun 195 hours, 18 minutes and 21 seconds earlier. President Nixon, waiting aboard the *Hornet* to greet them, hailed their achievement with obvious enthusiasm. At the same time, more than 4,000 miles away in Houston's Mission Control, nerve center of the flight, the words of John F. Kennedy's 1961 pledge flashed on a display board. Nearby, a smaller screen carried Apollo 11's *Eagle* emblem along with the immensely proud statement: "Task accomplished ... July 1969."

Twelve Months, 12 Men, Four Historic Voyages

The Apollo 11 moon landing was only the highlight of a banner year for NASA

In 1969 NASA's Apollo program was in high gear, driving toward the goal of putting men on the moon before 1970. The historic moon landing was made possible by the success of two previous missions that year, and it was followed by a second manned mission to the moon in November.

Apollo 9

Dates: March 3 to 13, 1969
Crew: Jim McDivvit, Mission Commander (MC); David Scott, Command Module (CM) pilot; Rusty Schweickart, Lunar Module (LM) pilot

The mission was designed to test the LM, christened *Spider,* and perfect its docking and undocking procedures with CM *Gumdrop.* It included spacewalks to test the backpack life-support systems designed for the moon landing. In addition, it was only the second manned flight for the mighty Saturn V rocket. After the crew completed 97% of their assigned tasks in the first five days of the mission, NASA kept them aloft for another five days to test the reliability of the Apollo systems and to practice navigation and guidance. The most trying moments of the journey came after splash-down, when rough Pacific winds and waves added drama to the process of retrieving the astronauts.

Apollo 10

Dates: May 18 to 26, 1969
Crew: Thomas Stafford, MC; John Young, CM pilot; Eugene Cernan, LM pilot

The Apollo 10 mission was an elaborate dress rehearsal for the actual moon landing. Once in lunar orbit, Stafford and Cernan successfully separated the LM *(Snoopy)* from the CM *(Charlie Brown),* then descended to some 47,000 ft. above the moon—as TIME's headline declared, "Nine Miles from the Goal." The veteran astronauts sent enthusiastic reports back to Earth. Zooming over the moon, Cernan exclaimed, "We're right there! We're right over it! I'm telling you, we are low; we're close, babe. This is it!"

Apollo 11

Dates: July 16 to 24, 1969
Crew: Neil Armstrong, MC; Michael Collins, CM pilot; Edwin (Buzz) Aldrin, LM pilot

"The members of Apollo 11's crew are seasoned, imperturbable astronauts," TIME informed its readers. Ohio-born Navy man Armstrong, an inscrutable loner, survived a series of close calls in his long career as a pilot, and flew Gemini 8 to the first successful space docking. Aldrin, a hard-driving West Point graduate and Air Force Academy faculty member from New Jersey with a doctorate from M.I.T., set the record for spacewalking (5 hr. 30 min.) during the four-day 1966 flight of Gemini 12. Collins, the most relaxed and outgoing of the three, was a West Point graduate who helped steer Gemini 10 through complicated rendezvous and docking maneuvers.

Apollo 12

Dates: Nov. 14 to 24, 1969
Crew: Charles Conrad Jr., MC; Richard Gordon Jr., CM pilot; Alan Bean, LM pilot

How quickly we forget: "Four months after the historic flight of Apollo 11," TIME noted in November 1969, as Apollo 12 launched, "much of the mystery and tension that accompanied man's first landing on the moon seemed to be missing." Maybe so, but the Apollo 12 crew made a pinpoint landing in the Ocean of Storms and set up a complex research station, though a TV camera intended to show their moonwalks failed.

APOLLO 10 CREW: *From left, Cernan, Young, Stafford*

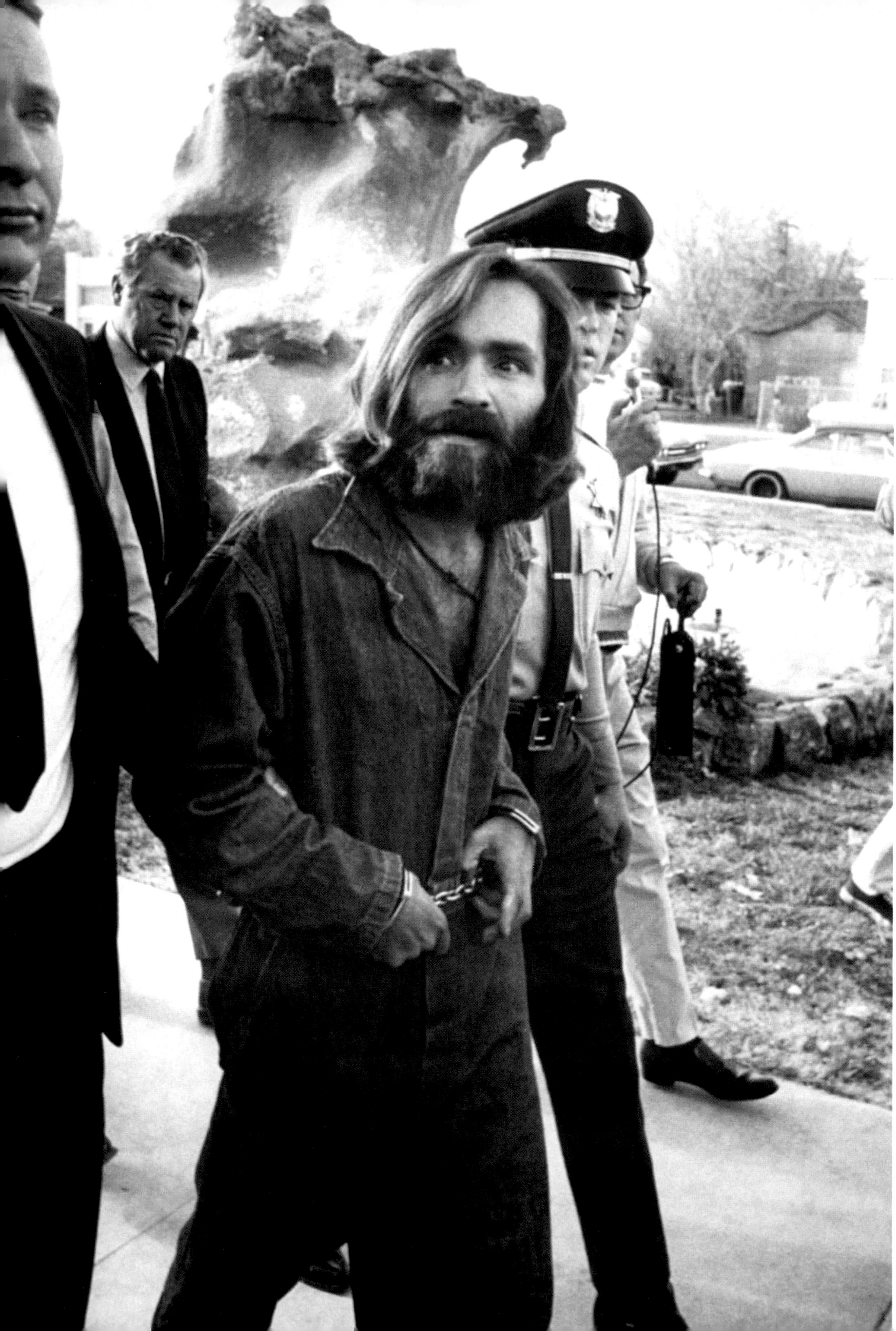

VERNON MERRITT III—TIME LIFE PICTURES

Murder sans motive *Above, Los Angeles police examine a corpse on the lawn of the Polanski-Tate home. At left, Manson is arraigned in Los Angeles, after being transferred from a local jail in Independence, Calif.*

High on Homicide

The murders of a crazed guru's "Family" terrorize Los Angeles

THE CRIME WAS 'SO WEIRD AND BIZARRE,' DECLARED Los Angeles coroner Thomas Noguchi, that he had taken an unusual step," TIME reported in its issue of Aug. 22, 1969. "He was showing photographs of the bodies of starlet Sharon Tate and four other murder victims to a psychologist and a psychiatrist. Perhaps the killer had left some clue to his character in his sick and savage assault on the bodies of his victims."

Weird and bizarre, sick and savage: those words only begin to convey the horror of what police found when summoned by a housekeeper to the Benedict Canyon home of Tate, 26, wife of Polish-born film director Roman Polanski, 36, on the morning of Aug. 9, 1969. But it would be a full four months—a period during which Angelenos would live in fear for their lives—before the full story of the night's quintuple murders would be revealed. And when they came to light, the facts of the case were so unusual as to sound like fiction.

The five victims, as well as a husband and wife slain in an equally bloody dual homicide that took place the following night, had been chosen almost at random. They were murdered not by a single person but by the followers of a hippie guru who maintained a "Family" of brainwashed, cultish devotees on a ramshackle movie-set dude ranch outside Los Angeles. The guru, Charles Manson, had not taken part in the actual murders but ordered them to be performed as a show of fealty by his all-too-willing followers. And his motive, L.A. prosecuting attorney Vincent Bugliosi would argue in his trial, was a half-baked conspiracy theory involving an apocalyptic race war and the overthrow of American society—all as communicated in secret to Manson via clues hidden in songs by the Beatles.

Sadly, the story of the Manson Family murders is also a tale of police bungling on an epic scale, as laid out in Bugliosi's classic account of the murders and the trial

The Victims
They died by chance, linked by Manson's hopes of creating a reign of terror in Los Angeles

Sharon Tate The up-and-coming movie star was a sexy, fresh-faced beauty who married Polish director Roman Polanski—known for his dark, macabre films—early in 1968. Above, one of their wedding pictures. She was an outgoing lover of nature who was thrilled with her pregnancy, friends said.

Jay Sebring The popular and successful Hollywood hair stylist had once been engaged to Sharon Tate but remained friendly with her after she married Polanski. The Polanskis introduced him to their friends, Frykowski and Folger.

Abigail Folger The heiress to the Folger's coffee fortune and boyfriend Frykowski had been introduced by novelist Jerzy Kosinski. They were staying at the house to keep Sharon Tate company while Polanski was filming in Europe.

Voityck Frykowski A close friend of Roman Polanski's from Poland, Frykowski had hopes of being a writer. He began dating the wealthy Folger in 1968. The two dined with Tate and Sebring at a Mexican restaurant the night of the murders.

Steven Parent The recent high school graduate had befriended the Tate house caretaker, William Garretson, and was visiting him in hopes of selling a used radio when he fell into the path of the killers, who shot him in his car.

Leno and Rosemary LaBianca The son of Italian immigrants, Leno was a successful second-generation grocer. He married Rosemary in 1960; it was the second marriage for both. They may have died simply because a Manson acquaintance lived near them in Los Feliz, and Family members knew the neighborhood.

that followed, *Helter Skelter* (W.W. Norton; 1974).

When police and coroner Noguchi were summoned to the Tate home, they found five dead bodies, several of them horribly butchered. The body of Steven Parent, 18, was found in a car in the front driveway, shot four times. Inside the house were the bodies of Tate and Jay Sebring, 35, a hair stylist. Tate had been stabbed deeply 16 times by a knife. She had been more than eight months pregnant, and the child she carried was also dead. Sebring had been shot and stabbed seven times. On the lawns outside the house, police found two more bodies. Abigail Folger, 25, a close Tate friend, had been stabbed 28 times. Her boyfriend, Polish-born Voityck Frykowski, 32, had been hit on the head repeatedly with a gun butt, shot twice and stabbed 51 times.

In addition to the frightful violence, the crime scene presented other unusual aspects. Most chillingly, the word PIG had been scrawled in human blood on the front door of the house. Money was found in the bedrooms and on the victims' bodies, indicating that robbery had not been a motive. However, as TIME reported, "Rumors of a wild drug and liquor spree were set off when police found a small quantity of marijuana and other drugs [cocaine] in Sebring's black Porsche ... Theories of sex, drug and witchcraft cults spread quickly in Hollywood, fed by the fact that Sharon [Tate] and Polanski circulated in one of the film world's more offbeat crowds." Such theories were shared by the police, who also found marijuana and hashish within the residence. In a classic case of blaming the victims, police immediately assumed that the crimes were the result of drug abuse, a drug deal gone bad or some sort of deviant occult or sexual ritual.

Los Angeles was still reeling from shock and spreading rumors about the gruesome Tate murders when a second multiple murder occurred, only nine miles away and 24 hours later. Leno LaBianca, 44, the owner of four markets, and his wife Rosemary, 38, were slashed to death in their secluded home in the Los Feliz area. "It's a carbon copy," reported a policeman upon first viewing the scene, and fears of a maniac running amuck quickly spread through the city. Indeed, there were chilling similarities between the two slaughters: the words DEATH TO PIGS had been smeared in blood on a wall of the LaBianca home, along with the words HEALTER-SKELTER (sic), and the victims' bodies had been mutilated. Leno had been stabbed 26 times by a knife and a carving fork; his wife had been stabbed 41 times. Tate and Sebring had been found with a nylon rope wrapped around their necks; lamp cords were wrapped around the LaBiancas' necks.

W HAT HAPPENED NEXT STILL BEGGARS BELIEF: despite the obvious similarities between the two crimes, TIME reported, "On more thorough investigation, the Los Angeles police decided that the similarities were largely superficial—and perhaps intentional—and that the crimes were probably unconnected except by the publicity given the first one." As a result, two separate teams of detectives were assigned to the cases.

Authorities bungled the case in other ways. The troubles began from the moment L.A. police arrived at the Tate residence: fingerprints were smeared, physical evidence scattered, blood samples compromised, major evidence overlooked. When a Van Nuys boy found the gun used in the Tate murders, he turned it into the local station house, where it remained unexamined for months, a short distance from the two detective teams.

The case was finally broken, not by police work but because murderer, Susan Atkins, 21, boasted about the killings to fellow inmates after she and 24 other Family members were arrested in a raid involving car thefts rather than the Tate murders. When she was interrogated, the story of the bizarre world of Charles Manson and his self-styled Family began to take shape.

Atkins sketched out a weird story of a mystical, semi-religious hippie drug-and-murder cult led by the bearded, charismatic Manson, who dispatched his zombic-like followers, mostly girls wearing hunting knives, on "creepy crawl" missions in affluent Los Angeles neigh-

Ranch Days
The Family's hideaway

Charles Manson began to gather his Family in San Francisco's Haight-Ashbury district in 1967, and in 1968 he moved his retinue by bus to Los Angeles to further his music-writing ambitions, holing up at a 500-acre dude ranch in western Los Angeles County owned by octogenarian George Spahn. The old man, played for a fool by Manson's young female followers, agreed to house the guru and his crew for free. Here Manson busied himself converting stolen cars into dune buggies, pursuing his musical dreams (with no success) and ordering Family members to conduct "creepy crawl" commando forays into affluent neighborhoods.

Shortly after the murders, police raided the ranch and took Manson and a few others into custody for car theft, but they were set free because the search warrant had not been filed properly, and Manson then led his followers to a new camp in Independence, Calif., near Death Valley. Here, among the greasewood and rattlesnakes, they holed up in run-down cabins and led an indolent, almost savage existence, singing Manson's songs, stealing cars for cash and picking through garbage for food. Once again, Manson was picked up for car theft, and he was in a local jail when he was first linked to the Tate-LaBianca murders.

SPAHN RANCH *The Manson Family was holed up here at the time of the Tate-LaBianca murders; they later moved to Death Valley*

The Killers

They had never even met their
victims, yet they murdered them
in exceptionally violent fashion

Susan Atkins, Patricia Krenwinkel, Leslie Van Houten The three women defendants, shown above entering court in August 1970, remained firmly in Manson's thrall during the trial, showing no remorse for their ultra-violent crimes. When Manson carved an X-sign into his forehead as a sign of his persecution by society, they quickly followed suit. All were given death sentences, later commuted to life imprisonment, and are still incarcerated in California. (Van Houten was convicted in the LaBianca killings; she was not present at the Tate murders.) All have now expressed their repentance for their crimes. As of spring 2009, Susan Atkins had been diagnosed with terminal brain cancer and was not expected to survive until 2010.

Linda Kasabian Shown at right at her arraignment in Los Angeles in December 1969, Kasabian, was five months pregnant and was the mother of a 2-year-old. She turned state's evidence and was the key witness in the case in exchange for immunity, testifying that she had been present at both murder scenes but had not taken part in the crimes.

Charles Watson "Tex," as he was known in the Manson Family, was tried separately from the other defendants. He was the lead killer at both murder scenes, and he later admitted he told victim Voityck Frykowski, "I'm the devil and I'm here to do the devil's business." As with the other killers, his death sentence was commuted to life imprisonment. Now a born-again Christian living in a California state prison, he claims he has repented for his deeds.

borhoods. Such secretive raids led to Manson's later commands to his followers to commit eight murders in the late summer of 1969. (Further revelations would tie the Manson Family to a number of other murders.)

Manson, Atkins told police, had ordered the Tate murders on Aug. 9 and those of the LaBiancas on Aug. 10. He had also ordered an earlier murder that had remained unsolved: that of musician Hinman on July 25. Hinman was murdered, Atkins alleged, because he would not turn over $20,000 that Manson thought he had recently come into.

The victims at Tate's home, Atkins admitted, did not even know Manson: they died because Manson, an aspiring songwriter, nursed a grudge against actor Doris Day's son, Terry Melcher, a record producer who had earlier refused to have one of Manson's songs recorded. Polanski and Tate had rented the Melcher house, and Manson ordered everyone in it killed, presumably not even knowing who the tenants at the time were—or caring. Atkins told police that she was present but did not participate in the murders.

According to Atkins, she and fellow Family members Charles Watson, 23, Linda Kasabian, 20, and Patricia Krenwinkel, 22, entered Tate's house and stabbed and shot the four victims. The pregnant Tate, she reported, pleaded, "Please, let me have my baby," but was violently hacked to death. Before entering the Tate house, Watson had shot Parent in his car; he had been preparing to leave after visiting an acquaintance, caretaker William Garretson, in a separate cottage behind the home.

The LaBiancas, Atkins stated, were picked at random from among the affluent, the night after the Tate murders, just to prove that the killers had not lost their nerve—and to keep Manson's supposed "Helter Skelter" revolution alive. Manson had been present at the LaBianca home and had helped tie up the couple, then had left the killing to Watson, Krenwinkel and Family member Leslie Van Houten, 19. Acting on Atkins' statement, police quickly arrested Watson, Krenwinkel and Kasabian. Ironically, Manson was already in police custody at the time; he was being held on car-theft charges in Independence, Calif., near Death Valley, where he had led his Family after the August murder sprees. He was brought to Los Angeles and arraigned on Dec. 11.

After she was allowed to meet briefly with Manson behind bars early in 1970, Atkins immediately recanted the accounts she had given, claiming they had been fabricated. Manson's hold over her remained strong. Prosecutor Bugliosi then turned to Family member Kasabian, who agreed to testify against Manson and the murderers in exchange for immunity.

"I have stayed in jail and I have stayed stupid, and I have stayed a child while I have watched your world grow up and then I look at the things you do and I don't understand. I have done my best to get along in your world, and now you want to kill me. I say to myself, 'Ha, ha, I'm already dead, have been all my life.'"

—CHARLES MANSON, COURT STATEMENT

THE TRIAL THAT FOLLOWED WAS OF A PIECE WITH the Manson Family's crimes; from the beginning, it unspooled like a species of absurdist theater. Manson played the role of a psychotic madman, frequently interrupting the trial with nutty outbursts. A posse of his female followers who had not been charged with the crimes watched the trial inside the courtroom, joined Manson in his frequent interruptions of the process and kept vigil on a corner down the street from the courthouse, basking in the massive publicity the proceedings attracted. When Manson entered the courtroom one day with a scar shaped like an X on his forehead, his devotees followed suit; when he changed the X to a swastika, they did the same; when he shaved his head, so did his female followers.

The defense, in effect, was no defense at all. One of the Family's court-appointed attorneys, Ronald Hughes, disappeared during the trial. His body was not discovered until the trial's end; he is believed to have been killed by Family members, but no charges were ever filed. The lawyers representing the defendants had no outside witnesses to help their case and were afraid to put the women on the stand, believing that they would take full responsibility for the killings to absolve Manson. As a result, after the prosecution presented its case over a period of more than three months, the defense rested, without bringing a single witness to the stand.

The jury found Manson and his three female followers guilty, and on March 29, 1971, they were sentenced to death. The sentences were reduced to life in prison when, in 1972, the California Supreme Court outlawed the death penalty. Charles Watson, the Family member who was the lead killer in both multiple murders, was tried separately and found guilty in October 1971. Forty years later, four of the five defendants found guilty have confessed to their crimes and expressed their remorse. Charles Manson, 74 in 2009, has never done so.

The Leader
A life gone wrong ends in mind control and murders

Born in 1934 in Ohio to an unwed teenage mother, Charles Manson never saw his father. His prostitute parent was often in jail, and young Manson was shifted around from relatives to foster parents to reformatories. He soon turned to crime, mainly car theft. His education never went beyond the seventh grade. By the time he was 32, he had spent 16 years in jails or reformatories. Along the way he had become interested in music and the occult, and after his release from a federal prison in March, 1967, he headed for San Francisco. As a "roving minstrel" in the Summer of Love, he soon found an abundance of young innocents, mainly women, who were eager for guidance. The Family had begun to form.

By 1969, relocated to Los Angeles, Manson held an almost hypnotic spell over a band of 30 or more followers, who called him "God" and "Satan." He was much older than the young women he attracted, many of whom had been victims of sexual abuse or were runaways. Adept at programming his charges, Manson charmed his serfs with rambling, mystical speechifying and pretensions of spiritual grandeur, and broke down their inhibitions by dispensing psychedelic drugs freely, encouraging casual nudity and stage-managing elaborate orgies. The Manson Family resembled a seraglio, as the female followers of the self-proclaimed "Son of Man," often nude or barebreasted, catered to his every whim.

Manson was sentenced to death in 1971, but the California Supreme Court soon outlawed the death penalty. He remains incarcerated in California state prisons, denied parole 11 times as of 2007. The photo above of Manson at age 74 was released in March 2009; it was taken as part of a routine visual survey of prisoners.

DAWN'S EARLY LIGHT: *Above, Jimi Hendrix; at right, fans pour into the festival site, eventually numbering some 400,000*

Peace, Love and Mud

Q: Was it the dawning of the Age of Aquarius—or merely the dawning of four decades of baby boomer self-infatuation? A: Yes

THE SPONTANEOUS COMMUNITY OF YOUTH THAT was created at Bethel [N.Y.] was the stuff of which legends are made," TIME wrote the week after the Woodstock "Aquarian Exposition" ended, and 40 years later, the legend machine is still humming at high speed. Woodstock, it turns out, is not only the stuff of which myths are made; it's the stuff of which 3-hr. Oscar-winning documentary films, top-selling albums, hit singles, artistic reputations, a host of cable-TV retrospectives, a zillion baby-boomer boasts and a $100 million museum are made.

The Woodstock Museum is the brainchild of Cablevision founder Alan Gerry, who bought more than 2,000 acres of farmland on and near the festival site and in 2008 opened an outdoor performance stage and a mu-

seum crammed with interactive displays, a faux-hippie bus and a gift shop. As further proof that Woodstock hasn't lost its mojo, when supporters sought federal funding for the museum, four decades vanished in a flash, and stern-faced, finger-wagging U.S. Congressmen took turns denouncing the project as a monument to hippies and a flashback on bad acid. The funding was defeated 52 to 42 in the U.S. Senate. Bummer!

The debate over the legacy of Woodstock is also still raging in a medium that didn't exist when the festival celebrated its 30th anniversary in 1999: YouTube. Thanks to this user-supported video archive, it's easy to retrieve footage of the event, from the performances of individual bands to outtakes from the *Woodstock* documentary film to home movies shot on outdated equip-

HOME OF THE RAVE *Early arrivals set up camp. Hippies loved displaying the flag to prove they were as patriotic as "straights"*

ment. But once you've gazed your fill at the self-styled "freaks" who came together so memorably at Bethel, take a look at the YouTube viewers' comments, and you'll find that many people refuse to view the legendary love-in through rose-colored glasses, much less the purple haze of an acid trip.

"Thank God this time is over, and taped on DVD, so we can consume it with a large burger from McDonald's," writes one skeptical viewer. "Young people are a little more realistic today, in the sense that they are very conscious about the most important things in the world: health, status and money." Another viewer begs to differ: "Ideas like love, sharing, community, cooperation, green ecology, clean energy, tolerance, diversity … all of that was not pathetic."

And so on. Yet why all the fuss over a 40-year-old rock concert? "When the legend becomes fact, print the legend," a character observes in John Ford's brilliant study of mythmaking on the Western frontier, *The Man Who Shot Liberty Valance.* But when an event has become as encrusted in lore as Woodstock, it can help to simply recall a few basic facts. So here goes:

Woodstock, essentially a triumph of improvisation, barely got off the ground in the first place. Moneymen

John Roberts and Joel Rosenman, who teamed with the more music-oriented duo of Michael Lang and Artie Kornfeld to promote the event, originally reserved outdoor space for the festival in Wallkill, N.Y., but when town elders got wind of what awaited them, they revoked the festival permit. Via the recommendation of a mutual friend, the promoters eventually rented 600 acres of land outside the small town of Bethel, N.Y., from a free-spirited farmer, Max Yasgur.

The promoters promised Yasgur that 50,000 people would attend. Oops—their bad! As word of the concert's roster of stars and countrified location began to spread among the hundreds of thousands of college kids winding up summer vacations along the East Coast—well, "Road trip!" Those in the wider hippie vanguard around the nation, including "heads" from the Hog Farm commune and writer Ken Kesey's renowned Merry Pranksters, also made tracks for upstate New York.

By Friday afternoon, Aug. 15, as performer Arlo Guthrie would inform the crowd from the stage, the New York State Thruway was so jammed with traffic that it was shut down. Eventually, festivalgoers, many without tickets, abandoned their cars by the side of the road and headed for Yasgur's farm. Though the site had been

O say, can you see? *In search of a better view, fans climb up a speaker tower. After all, Woodstock was all about getting higher*

surrounded by a chain-link fence, there was no controlling a crowd of this size. As thousands of kids breached the fence, the promoters wisely decided to open the event to all. Woodstock had become a free festival.

Now what? Imagine you planned a party for 50,000 people—and 400,000 showed up. You would be deficient in all basic services, from porta-potties to food to water to police presence. The festive freaks soon found, to their amazement, that they had landed in hippie Nirvana: with no parents or authority figures in sight, it was party time. Use of such illegal drugs as pot and LSD, well hidden in normal life, was rampant. The warning from the stage—"Stay away from the brown acid"—became a punch line that's still tossed around.

BUT SURPRISE, SURPRISE: PROVING THAT PEACE, love and good vibes can sustain an instant community for at least a few days, the festival proceeded with very few incidents of violence or unrest. It's believed that two people died, one the victim of a heroin overdose, the other a sleeping camper accidentally run over by a tractor. And when the rains came, drenching everyone on Sunday afternoon? Well, when life handed them mud, Woodstock Nation's citizens made mudslides—whee! It is this sense of community and unified improvisation that primarily accounts for the event's magical afterglow. A massive group of people came together in a determined effort to overcome every obstacle thrown at them—from bad planning to bad weather to bad acid—and *laissez les bon temps roulez.*

Oh, yeah: What about the music? Though the stage show ran hours behind its announced schedule, standout acts like the Who, Joe Cocker, Santana and a new supergroup performing for only the second time in public, Crosby, Stills and Nash (with Neil Young sitting in), simply wowed the crowd. The last performer, who electrified sleepy fans in the early hours of Monday morning, was guitar god Jimi Hendrix. His distorted, triumphant rendition of *The Star-Spangled Banner* remains the national anthem of Woodstock Nation.

The most notorious confrontation at the festival occurred onstage, of all places. When Yippie rabble-rouser Abbie Hoffman spotted two things he couldn't resist—an open microphone and an audience of 400,000—he attempted to commandeer Who leader Pete Townshend's mike, upon which Townshend whacked him hard with his electric guitar and advised him, "(Get the) f--- off my f---ing stage." Peace out, brother.

ELLIOT LANDY—MAGNUM PHOTOS

Flashbacks

Yes, it was primarily a music festival, but Woodstock was a feast for both eyes and ears

GET THIS PARTY STARTED *Veteran folk artist Richie Havens led off the festival on Friday afternoon. The promoters engaged a surprisingly wide variety of performers, introducing such little-known groups as the Incredible String Band and the energetic '50s-revival act Sha-na-na to a huge new audience. At left, an entranced Havens is still strumming as he heads backstage*

FREE AT LAST *The crowd grooves to the music. Festivalgoers were stunned at the novel feeling of so many "freaks"—the hippies' ironic term for themselves—gathered together in one place. Within months, Yippie Abbie Hoffman published a book hailing* Woodstock Nation

VERY MERRY *Writer Ken Kesey's famed psychedelic bus arrived from San Francisco, but the head Prankster wasn't onboard*

WHEN THE RAIN COMES *Who needs an umbrella when you've got a smile, a piece of plastic and a tambourine?*

REEFER MADNESS *This banner on a paraphernalia tent is both invitation and advertisement, and we suspect the substance to be inhaled was not tobacco. With local authorities overwhelmed by the crowd, the festival was essentially self-policed*

NO SHIRT, NO PROBLEM *Many at the festival skinny-dipped in a nearby stream; others stopped just this side of nudity*

DUDE! *Artist and Merry Prankster Paul Foster sports full hippie regalia; Jerry Garcia walks behind him*

JOE COCKER *Little known before Woodstock, the British rocker thrilled the crowd with his guttural vocals and spastic moves*

RAVI SHANKAR *The Indian master, famous for tutoring Beatle George Harrison on sitar, rocked out on a raga*

HARMONIOUS *Graham Nash and David Crosby, of then-new group Crosby, Stills and Nash, reach for the high notes*

JEFFERSON AIRPLANE *With the Grateful Dead, the Airplane, with singers Grace Slick and Marty Balin front and center, represented the San Francisco psychedelic sound at Woodstock. Just weeks after the festival, the group began recording its* Volunteers *album, which reflected a newly radical political stance*

THE WHO *The British group's highly polished sound was a contrast to the looser, boogie-based American bands. Their soaring anthems, instrumental virtuosity and strong stage presence made their set, featuring songs from the rock opera* Tommy, *a highlight of the festival*

WHO'S ON FIRST? *Little seemed to faze the festival's promoters, including Michael Lang, center. When he and partners John Roberts, Joel Rosenman and Artie Kornfeld realized they had lost control of access to the site, they wisely declared the event a "free festival" and created a safe, memorable experience from a situation that could easily have degenerated into chaos*

JANIS JOPLIN *The blues belter from east Texas, who performed as a solo act with a backing band, appears to have exchanged her usual Southern Comfort for some French bubbly backstage*

Swan Songs of the '60s

All hail swamp rock, funk, Motown—and the return of the King

BACK ON TOP *Fresh from his triumphant 1968 "comeback special" on TV, a rejuvenated Elvis Presley, 34, returned to live performing after a 13-year hiatus. On July 31, 1969,* TIME *reported, "He stepped onstage in front of a gold lamé curtain at Las Vegas' new International Hotel, coordinated his pelvic girdle and his phallic guitar, closed his eyes, tossed his head and sent a solar wind of nostalgia over the 2,000 middle-aged record executives, hotel guests and show folks assembled for opening night … After an especially rabid* Hound Dog *that ended with a split-kick jump, he was so winded that he reached for a glass of water, telling the audience, 'You just look at me for a couple of minutes while I get my breath back.' " Above, "the King" poses with his queen, 24-year-old Priscilla Presley, later in 1969 in California. The two had wed on May 1, 1967.*

BORN ON THE BAYOU? *Not really—the members of Creedence Clearwater Revival hailed from California. Then again, the Beach Boys didn't surf much either. In 1969, CCR came out of nowhere to top the charts with the massive hits* Proud Mary *and* Bad Moon Rising. TIME *hailed leader John Fogerty's swamp-rock band for their "lean, masculine sound, impeccable instrumental style and express-track delivery."*

SLY? YES. STONED? PROBABLY *Sylvester (Sly) Stone and his bandmates, including brother Freddie and sister Rose, sang* "I Want to Take You Higher," *to the vast crowd at Woodstock—and in one of the festival's strongest performances, they did. The integrated band, whose music mixed, matched and improved upon a variety of styles—funk, acid rock, jazz, Motown—released their classic album* Stand! *in May 1969.*

THE JACKSON FIVE *Some people are just born to be at center stage, and even at age 11, it was Michael Jackson who occupied the pivotal position among his four siblings on this 1969 TV show. From left, that's Tito, Marlon, Michael, Jackie and Jermaine. After signing with Motown Records, the family band from Gary, Ind., had a monster success with the single* I Want You Back *in 1969.*

AFTERMATH *Camille's monster winds flattened homes and trees in this neighborhood of Biloxi, Miss..*

Colossal Camille Batters the Gulf
One of the strongest hurricanes on record devastates Mississippi

MOVE OVER, KATRINA—1969'S HURRICANE CA-mille remains the second most intense tropical storm ever to make landfall in the U.S. since the era of modern hurricane measurement began in the 1930s. (The strongest? The Labor Day Hurricane of 1935, which occurred before meteorologists began assigning alphabetical names to the big tropical storms, in 1950.) Camille crossed the Atlantic Ocean from Africa, moved through the Caribbean and grazed the west coast of Cuba, where it killed three people. As the storm neared the U.S. coast, instruments on oil rigs measured the waves it generated at 44 ft. (13 m) in height. It slammed into the U.S. Gulf Coast near Bay St. Louis, Miss., on the night of Aug. 17 as a Category 5 storm with winds exceeding 190 m.p.h., devastating the entire Mississippi coast and dealing heavy blows to Louisiana and Alabama. It then continued moving

north and east, unleashing torrential rains, until it looped east and headed out to the Atlantic again off the Virginia coast. The storm surge when Camille tore into the Mississippi coast was measured at 24 ft. (7 m).

As stunned rescue officials gathered damage reports in the days that followed, Camille's deadly impact was turned into statistics: 256 dead and $1.4 billion in damages (in 1969 dollars; the total today would surpass $9 billion). The storm's rain clouds proved as deadly as its winds: in hard-hit Nelson County, Va— which was inundated by 28 in. of rain in only 8 hours—flash floods and mudslides claimed 113 lives.

A TIME reporter visiting the Louisiana and Mississippi coasts in late November reported, "Both areas remain a jumble of devastation. Hundreds of homes, motels and other business establishments stand roofless or without walls. Uprooted trees, torn chunks of pave-

TOPSY-TURVY *Camille blew boats onto a levee near Boothville, La., left, and tore down Rosemary Theriot's home in Biloxi, above*

ment and twisted iron fences bestrew the roadsides. Some families are living in tents on their front lawns."

"I came into this world with nothing," Herman W. Ryals, a retired civil service worker, told TIME, "and it looks as though that's the way I'm going to leave it." Nothing remained of the disabled man's modest frame home near the beach at Gulfport, Miss., the magazine reported, and he and his wife were living in a leased trailer on their hurricane-stripped lot. His insurance company offered to pay only 25% of his claim, Ryals said, so he had hired a lawyer to sue for more. In the interim the lender was threatening to foreclose the mortgage that covered his lot and vanished home. Most property insurance, coastal residents were learning to their chagrin, covered wind, rain or lightning damage, but not destruction caused by high tides or waves.

Insurance companies may not have changed much

in four decades, but the expectations of the Federal Government's response to such national disasters have certainly ramped up. In 1969 the federal agency that responded to such disasters was the Federal Disaster Assistance Administration, an underfunded arm of the relatively new Department of Housing and Urban Development, which attempted—and often failed—to coordinate the response of more than 100 state, federal and civilian agencies. And it was not until late in September, six weeks after the killer storm made landfall, that President Richard Nixon arrived in Gulfport, Miss., to view the damage. He was met by an exuberant, cheering crowd of some 30,000 people at the Gulfport airport—a reflection, TIME reported, not of his presence in response to the massive disaster but of the pioneering "Southern Strategy" of his Republican Party, which had made Nixon highly popular in the South.

ACCELERATOR *Andretti strikes a pose with an open-wheel car in Phoenix in 1969, one of the best years of his storied career*

Mario Andretti

He began racing as a youngster in Italy—and he hasn't slowed down since

WHEN DIMINUTIVE (5 FT. 6 IN.), ITALIAN-BORN Mario Andretti first roared onto the U.S. racing scene in the mid-1960s, even those who admired him begged him to slow down a bit—and to stop racing so many kinds of cars. Both his schedule and his tactics were suicidal, critics said. "Sometimes you should wait to pass," veteran driver Parnelli Jones told TIME, "and Mario often doesn't." Two-time Indy 500 Winner Rodger Ward agreed, saying, Andretti "has to learn patience; he tries to overpower the competition."

Andretti, who seemed to harbor the weird notion that overpowering the competition was the goal of racing in the first place, fired back. "I don't have any feeling of accomplishment about anything unless there's a lot of risk to it," he told TIME in 1967. And why race only one kind of car, when there were so many interesting ways to get from here to there in a hurry? You name it, Mario drove it: Indy cars, stock cars, sports cars, Formula One cars, midget racers, sprint cars. In 1965, as a raw rookie at the Indianapolis 500, he astounded racing experts by placing third and winning $42,551. In 1969 he won for the first time at Indy. It was only one highlight of what proved a banner year for Andretti, who turned 29 that February: he won eight additional races on the IndyCar circuit, won the Pikes Peak International Hill Climb, and was named Athlete of the Year by ABC's *Wide World of Sports*.

Andretti would continue to test himself on every kind of track and in every kind of car: he is the only driver in history to win the Daytona 500 (1967), Indianapolis 500 (1969) and Formula One World Championship (1978). Ironically, after 1969 he never again won at Indy's famous Brickyard: his later career there—as well as that of his son Michael—has been so plagued by misfortune and goofy setbacks that racing fans have a name for it: Andretti's Curse.

Tom Seaver

In his third year in the league, a young pitcher leads the Mets to glory

ON THE NIGHT OF JULY 9, 1969, TOM SEAVER, who at only 24 was the hard-throwing ace of the New York Mets pitching staff, put on the most dazzling one-man show in his team's previously dismal history: he faced just 28 Chicago Cubs batters to achieve a 4-0 victory. Only a line single by Rookie Jim Qualls in the ninth inning spoiled Seaver's bid for what would have been the 11th perfect game in baseball history. But if Seaver didn't quite achieve perfection that night, he served notice that the team long regarded as the laughingstock of baseball was determined to win the World Series in 1969.

A few months later, it was the husky Seaver who prevailed over the Atlanta Braves' Phil Niekro, 9-5, to win the first game of the National League Championship Series. After the Mets advanced to the World Series, manager Gil Hodges called once again for "Tom Terrific" to pitch the first game—but Seaver, who had won a whopping 25 games during the regular season, was outpitched by the Baltimore Orioles' Mike Cuellar, and the Mets lost, 4-1. Unfazed, Seaver came back strong to win the fourth game of the Series, pitching 10 complete innings in a nail-biting 2-1 Mets victory.

Seaver was in only his third year in the major leagues in 1969, and he was still surprised at his success, he told TIME. Coming out of high school, the Californian had been regarded as too small even to play college ball, but six months of lifting crates in a warehouse and another six months of active duty in the Marine Reserves put 4 in. and 35 lbs. on his frame before he entered the University of Southern California, where his pitching also got stronger. After he topped out at 6 ft. 1 in. and 200 lbs., "people didn't even recognize me," he said. But they recognized his new prowess on the mound, where a blistering fastball joined his array of sliders and curves. A few years later, every baseball fan knew and respected Seaver, including the editors of SPORTS ILLUSTRATED, who named him Sportsman of the Year 1969.

HERE'S THE PITCH *When Tom Seaver met Nelson Rockefeller, governor of New York, they both ended up signing autographs*

CHAMPS! *Mets manager Gil Hodges traverses the ticker tape in Manhattan after the Series. Sadly, the beloved coach and player, whose career dated back to the glory days of the 1950s Brooklyn Dodgers, died from a heart attack in 1972 at age 47*

<small>KEN REGAN—CAMERA 5</small>

BUBBLING OVER *First baseman Ed Kranepool (No. 7) hoists the champagne in the locker room of the World Champion Mets*

Miracle of the Amazin' Mets

Baseball's storied laughingstocks go from worst to first

TO APPRECIATE HOW WONDROUSLY GOOD THE NEW York Mets were in 1969, you first must recall how wondrously bad every Mets team had been since the club's debut as a National League expansion squad in 1961. Coached by Casey Stengel, the legendary dugout philosopher and inventive practitioner of the English tongue, those first editions of the Mets were a congeries of castoffs who excelled at finding brilliantly creative ways to lose ballgames. A true Mets fan, TIME opined on the eve of the '69 World Series, "had to be a man of almost mystical forbearance, untrammeled optimism and infinite compassion for the inept ... Baseball, according to a hoary cliché, is a game of inches. The Mets lost by feet, even yards, and they did so with agonizing regularity ... [They were] incontestably the most ludicrous team in the chronicle of baseball."

But that was then. Now, in 1969, the Mets were, in a word that came to symbolize their season, Amazin'. Guided by steady manager Gil Hodges, the Mets' young

prodigies—including mound aces Tom Seaver, 24, Jerry Koosman, 25, and Nolan Ryan, 22—were the happiest, hungriest, hustlingest team in baseball. First, they stole the league championship away from the Chicago Cubs, who—brace yourself—collapsed at the end of the summer. Then they swept a strong Atlanta Braves team in three games to win the National League pennant.

But in the World Series, the Mets ran up against one of the great clubs of any era, the '69 Baltimore Orioles. Through their dugout strode such storied sluggers as outfielder Frank Robinson, third baseman Brooks Robinson and first baseman Boog Powell, as well as pitchers Jim Palmer and Mike Cuellar. In the first game, Seaver faltered and Cuellar pitched the Orioles to a 4-1 win. But that ended their highlight reel: the Amazin's swept the next four games behind the strong bats of outfielders Cleon Jones and Tommie Agee. The tramps were champs! And there was so much joy in New York City, they say you could hear it all the way to Mudville.

Classic Competitors

Bill, Rod and Maggie excel—and a Yankee says farewell

BATTLE OF THE TITANS *What's more classic than the Boston Celtics facing the Los Angeles Lakers in the NBA finals? That's easy: pit Bill Russell and Wilt Chamberlain against each other at center. That was the script for 1969's memorable seven-game championship series, as the two legends squared off in their final battle. The 6-ft. 10-in. Russell, left, in his last year in the game, was serving as player-coach. The 7-ft. 1-in. Chamberlain had dominated Russell in the finals only two years before, when his Philadelphia 76ers beat Boston, leading* TIME *to declare (prematurely) that the Celtics dynasty was over. But Boston took the '69 crown after Chamberlain suffered a knee injury in the seventh game and did not return to the court. Though most fans assumed the two great rivals disliked each other, Russell wrote a moving eulogy for* TIME *after Chamberlain died in 1999, revealing that the two had liked and respected each other as players and had become close friends in retirement.*

THE MICK HANGS IT UP *When he joined the New York Yankees back in 1951, the young man from Oklahoma was handed the tough task of replacing Joe DiMaggio. But Mickey Mantle soon proved he had the right stuff, bashing homers, chasing down long fly balls and speeding to run out well-placed bunts. After 18 years, the three-time American League* MVP *called it quits before the '69 season; he was honored with a special day at Yankee Stadium on June 8, 1969, when his number was retired.*

GRAND SLAM! *In 1969, men's tennis was divided into two leagues: Rod Laver—and everybody else. As* TIME *noted then, "At 31, 'the Rocket' (as Laver is persistently called) dominates his game more completely than any other athlete in the world." The hard-serving Aussie achieved a never equalled second Grand Slam in 1969 (his first was in 1962), winning the French, Australian and U.S. Opens as well as the Wimbledon title. Laver suffered a stroke in 1998, and he told* TIME *in 2008 that arthritis now keeps him off the court. Back in 1969, after winning the U.S. Open at Forest Hills, N.Y., Laver confided to* TIME *that he was motivated more by prize money than by the quest for glory. His check for winning: $16,000.*

HER MAJESTY *In an era when Australians dominated tennis, the queen of the courts was Margaret Court, 27 in 1969, who won three of the four major trophies that year—and would win all four in 1970. "A rangy country girl from New South Wales,"* said TIME, *"she overwhelms smaller players with her booming serves and bulleting volleys ... [but] the ardent gymnast and weight lifter bristles at the suggestion that she is some kind of Amazon in sneakers." At left, Court holds the British Hard Courts Championship trophy.*

THE GANG'S ALL HERE *There's no need to list these names—and that's the point. Like the characters from* The Brady Bunch, *the wonderfully human Muppets created by Jim Henson for* Sesame Street *have become woven into the fabric of American life*

Big Bird, a Bunch of Bradys and Tiny Tim

We said hello to a pair of kids' classics—and farewell to *Star Trek*

THE BIGGEST JUGGERNAUT IN THE HISTORY OF CHILdren's television sprang from mundane origins. At a Manhattan dinner party in 1966, a Carnegie Foundation executive named Lloyd Morrissett mentioned that his young daughter was so enthralled by television that she would park herself in front of the family's set to gaze at early-morning test patterns. That story prompted a public-television producer named Joan Ganz Cooney to investigate how television could be used to package education as entertainment: "What if it went down more like ice cream than spinach?"

The ensuing creation—in which kids learned everything from empathy to arithmetic under the tutelage of colorful creatures like an 8-ft.-tall canary and a misanthropic garbage-can dweller—was greeted with acclaim by parents and teachers and received a fan letter from President Richard Nixon. Four decades later, it's a cultural touchstone that remains required viewing for millions of youngsters in 120 countries.

Sesame Street burst into colorful life on the nation's TV screens with such revolutionary impact that within a year Big Bird himself was smiling out from the cover of TIME, as the magazine explored what had already become a phenomenon. "From the moment it was old enough to earn money, U.S. television has been squandering the country's greatest natural resource: the young audience," TIME asserted. "Until last year. Abruptly, the electronic babysitter moved onto a street called Sesame … the program proves that it is not only the best children's show in TV history, it is one of the best parents' shows as well."

Cooney and her Carnegie-funded organization, the Children's Television Workshop, enlisted Harvard University education expert Edward L. Palmer to help develop the show, and he worked with children across the country for 18 months, studying attention spans, areas of interest and eye movements. He and his researchers found that the most efficacious approach to learning used the fast switches of commercial TV, the quick cuts from animation to live action. Transitions were out, as were talking-head monologues delivered in stern tones by adults: too "Walter Cronkite."

And of course, there would be no Sesame Street without the genius of puppet master Jim Henson, whose Muppet creations for the show carry timeless appeal. Another pillar of the series, songwriter Joe Raposo, kept *Sesame Street* tunefully humming. And for those who don't care for electronic tutors, Cooney shared these reassuring words with TIME in that 1970 cover story: "TV has a very important role to play in education. Still, it's just a big cold box, and just can't replace a loving teacher who cares about a child."

MOTHER KNOWS BEST *Creator Cooney told* TIME *in 1970 that in its first shows,* Sesame Street *"was too tightly programmed to allow for surprises." Solution: loosen up*

THEY'RE PERFECT—YOU'RE NOT *At times, that seemed to be the central message of* The Brady Bunch, *the hit ABC comedy about a blended family (one all boys, one all girls) whose split-level home was generally buzzin' with merry mischief, wacky complications, happy endings and lessons learned. Big-T* TIME *was not kind to the show on its debut, saying it "was about a thousand decibels less hilariously amusing than [its] laughtrack suggested." But small-T time has been kinder: constantly in reruns and a beloved slice of Americana, the show remains the gold standard of family sitcoms and a much mocked, much loved TV classic.*

Illusion, Reality and a Split-Level Life

Maureen McCormick, 53, who portrayed Marcia Brady on The Brady Bunch, *reminisced with* TIME *in 2009. Her memoir,* Here's the Story *(William Morrow), was published in 2008.*

WHEN I FIRST GOT the news that I had been cast in *The Brady Bunch,* in early 1969, I was 13. Once it came out, I was embarrassed because it got terrible reviews. Everybody said it was totally unrealistic, which was true. After it became a hit, I was embarrassed because everybody said it was totally un-hip. Then, after it ended, I was embarrassed, because we were supposed to be so perfect. And that was so unreal, it made me wince.

The one aspect of the show that was real was that the cast became something like a genuine family. The child actors all became close friends. And Robert Reed was this loving father figure to all of us. The set was where we spent more time than at home with our actual families, so that became our real lives. But the relationships were also strangely different from a real family. I had a brief romance with Barry, who played my brother. Then Barry Williams had a major crush on Florence Henderson, who played our mother, and I fell in love with Reed, who played my father.

I had a really hard time separating myself from the character of Marcia, who was bigger than life. She was so perfect and happy, so sweet and wholesome. Meanwhile, I was struggling with depression. But nobody talked about that in the late 1960s, and I didn't realize that there was a history of it in my family. So I was deeply depressed, but I was hiding everything behind Marcia's smile. And everybody bought it.

I moved out of my family home when I was 17. Rebelling against the idealism of *The Brady Bunch* and looking for gritty reality, I went off the deep end and got heavily involved with drugs and trading sex for drugs. I realize now that I was trying to kill Marcia Brady. But the only way to really do that was to kill Maureen McCormick. Years later, I almost jumped off a hotel balcony. The things that saved me were my husband and family, the friends who stood by me, and finally getting into therapy and onto medication. My life today is something like a real-life version of *The Brady Bunch.* I'm happily married and have a well-adjusted child. But it's a more realistic, real-world version of that kind of happiness. Which is totally bizarre, I guess.

FINAL MISSION—NOT *On June 3, 1969, the final episode of the original* Star Trek *series aired on* NBC. *In its three-year run, the show failed to reach a wide audience, but it endured in reruns, mushrooming into a franchise whose latest incarnation, a film titled, simply,* Star Trek, *was released in May 2009.*

MUSICAL ROYALTY *On June 7, 1969,* The Johnny Cash Show *debuted on* ABC *with guests including Joni Mitchell and Bob Dylan, right—a coup for Cash as Dylan had never appeared on network TV and had been living in seclusion since 1966. Cash's now legendary show only aired until 1971, bringing to TV screens musicians who today are considered major talents but at the time were too esoteric for mainstream audiences.*

BELLS ARE RINGING *Talk about appointment TV: 40 million Americans tuned in to watch Tiny Tim, the helium-voiced professional eccentric and perennial Johnny Carson guest, marry his sweetheart, Miss Vicki (Victoria May Budinger), live on the* The Tonight Show *on Dec. 17, 1969. Although ukulele-playing musician Herbert Khaury, a.k.a. Tiny Tim, found fame as a novelty act and with his hit falsetto version of* Tiptoe Through the Tulips, *he was also a respected authority on the history of American and British popular song. He died in 1996, at age 64.*

UP AGAINST THE WALL *The trial was designed to suppress dissent but only fed its flames. Above, young protesters are detained by police outside the court building during the "Days of Rage" that accompanied the beginning of the trial on Oct. 11, 1969*

Show Trial of the Century

In Chicago, eight protesters—and American justice—stand trial

EFTY U.S. MARSHALS GUARDED THE ENTRANCES to Chicago's Federal Building, searching every package carried in and jostling anyone who did not move quickly enough toward the elevators. Other officers patrolled the aisles of the 23rd-floor courtroom. The black defendant sat chained to his chair by leg irons and handcuffs, emitting muffled obscenities toward the bench through a gag of muslin and tape. The jack-in-the-box jury scurried in and out of the chamber at the judge's direction, as outburst after outburst turned the proceedings into a bitter farce.

Despite the nightmare setting, this was no play by Jean Genet. It was, in fact, the deadly serious trial of eight radicals charged with conspiring to incite the riots that marred the Democratic National Convention in Chicago in 1968. The violent riots, shown live on TV while young protesters chanted "The whole world is watching!" had been one of the pivotal events of a cha-

otic year in which Martin Luther King Jr. and Robert F. Kennedy were assassinated, Lyndon Johnson decided to step down and Richard Nixon was elected President.

In December 1968 the Walker Commission, chartered by President Johnson to investigate the riots, submitted its findings. Titled *Rights in Conflict,* the report was based on 3,437 statements from eyewitnesses, as well as findings based on the viewing of some 180 hours of relevant film. While it depicted police as beset by foul-mouthed, obnoxious protesters, its final conclusion was unequivocal: "To read dispassionately the hundreds of statements describing at firsthand the events ... is to become convinced of the presence of what can only be called a police riot."

Case closed? Hardly. In Mayor Richard J. Daley's Chicago, there was no question that the police would not take sole blame for the messy civic meltdown. And President Nixon's new Attorney General, John Mitchell, was eager to clamp down on protest leaders. In March 1969 a federal grand jury in Chicago indicted eight demonstrators and eight Chicago policemen for their part in the disorders. (The eight police officers were tried separately: seven were acquitted and charges against one were dismissed.)

The men were the first to be charged under the 1968 Civil Rights Act for conspiring and crossing state lines to incite riot. The eight defendants were a carefully balanced grab bag of protest leaders, including two Yippies, a Black Panther, two academics, a longtime pacifist and other antiwar activists. As TIME noted, some of those indicted as "conspirators" had not met one another before they were indicted. Moreover, the magazine noted, "it might be said that the Chicago Eight are being tried for conspiring to incite the police to riot."

NO MATTER: IN THE WILD MONTHS THAT followed, the defendants turned the proceedings into a farce, eager to cast the event as little more than a politically motivated show trial. Mocking and cursing Judge Julius Hoffman and occasionally addressing the court at will, they employed tactics identical to those used on the streets during the convention riots, seeking to provoke Hoffman in the same way that demonstrators baited Chicago police into overreaction.

Mission accomplished. Hoffman, 74, tangled most severely with Black Panther Bobby Seale and ordered him restrained with handcuffs, leg irons and a gag, before finding him guilty of contempt of court and separating his case from those of the other seven. And the trial, far from putting a lid on dissent, kept the story in the headlines, stoked the fires of protest, undermined faith in the judicial system and created new martyrs for the antiwar cause.

In February 1970 all seven defendants were acquitted of the conspiracy charges, though five were found guilty of crossing state lines to incite a riot. They were fined $5,000 and sentenced to five years in jail. In 1972, the convictions were thrown out on appeal, and Judge Hoffman was reprimanded for his refusal to permit defense attorneys to screen prospective jurors for cultural and racial bias. The Justice Department chose not to request another trial. The '60s were exhausting enough to live through, without an instant replay.

The Chicago Eight

The men charged with conspiracy in the 1968 Chicago riots achieved national notoriety but had never been a unified group; they appear to have been selected to represent the range of protesters

David Dellinger The veteran peace activist, then 54, was an odd man out who chided the younger radicals for their hysterical rhetoric. He died in 2004.

Tom Hayden The gifted, mercurial writer and organizer, then 30, helped found the leftist Students for a Democratic Society. He later served in the California legislature and taught courses as a college professor.

Abbie Hoffman and Jerry Rubin were leaders of the prankishly absurdist Yippies, who brought a hippie ethos to politics. Hoffman, 33 in 1969, died in 1989; Rubin, 31 in 1969, died in 1994.

Rennie Davis, then 28, was the son of a White House economic adviser during the Truman Administration who worked as an organizer for the antiwar National Mobilization Committee. He later embraced Eastern religions.

John Froines, an assistant professor of chemistry at the University of Oregon, and **Lee Weiner,** a Northwestern University graduate student, represented antiwar activists from the academic world. Both were exonerated on all charges. Today Froines is director of the UCLA Center for Occupational and Environmental Health. Weiner remains active in social issues.

Bobby Seale The Black Panther leader, then 33, only came to the convention to fill in as a speaker for imprisoned fellow Panther Eldridge Cleaver. When his case was severed from that of the other defendants, the Chicago 8 became the Chicago 7. Today, Seale lectures on black history at universities across the U.S..

DOWN TO 7 *The defendants, after Bobby Seale's case was separated. From back left: Hoffman, Froines, Weiner, Dellinger, Davis and Hayden. Front row: Rubin and girlfriend Nancy Kurshan*

Massacre At My Lai

U.S. war crimes committed in 1968 are revealed
in 1969, kindling outrage—and regret

PLACE: QUANG NGAI PROVINCE, SOUTH VIETNAM. Date: March 16, 1968. Most of the young members of Charlie Company of the Americal Division's 11th Infantry Brigade had never been tested in direct combat with any large numbers of the enemy. Trained together in Hawaii, they had been in Vietnam only one month. Yet as part of Task Force Barker, their assignment in March was a fearsome one: to clear the Viet Cong out of Quang Ngai, an area long known as "the cradle of revolution" in Vietnam. The province had produced and harbored some of the Viet Minh's most effective fighters against the French in the 1950s and had been the target of the very first U.S. assault in the war. Yet it remained a stronghold of the V.C.'s 48th Local Force Battalion—an outfit with an eerie ability to disperse, then reappear to strike again.

The inexperienced Charlie Company, commanded by Captain Ernest Medina, 33, thus had ample cause for fear as it prepared to assault My Lai, a village with bricked-up huts and extensive hidden tunnels in an area called Pinkville (war maps showed population clusters like this group of nine hamlets in pink). The infantrymen were also angry. Repeatedly lashed by booby traps and sniper fire from unseen Viet Cong, the company's strength had already been cut from 190 to about 105. Of those, about 80 men were helicoptered into a grassy spot on the outskirts of My Lai on a warm, sunny morning.

Precisely what happened next has become one of the most notorious chapters of the U.S. intervention in Vietnam: a frenzy of murder on the part of U.S. serviceman that, if blessedly rare in the history of the American military, remains a horrifying example of the ways in which war can shatter basic precepts of conscience and honor. Initially, the events were hushed up by the U.S. Army in an investigation that amounted to a whitewash. But when reports of the My Lai massacre, as it has come to be known, reached the American public late in 1969, they unleashed a tsunami of national shame and self-examination. Like the Tet Offensive of early 1968, My Lai is regarded as a watershed in the bitter history of the war: a moment when the magnitude of the harm

Vᴉᴄᴛɪᴍs *Evidence of the massacre was captured by U.S. Army photographer Ronald Haeberle. When published in* Lɪꜰᴇ *magazine, the Cleveland* Plain Dealer *and* Der Stern *magazine in November 1969, the pictures ignited international outrage*

the conflict was inflicting on its victims—who in this case included not only the people of Vietnam but also the young American soldiers who had been dispatched in hopes of improving their lives—could no longer be denied.

That March morning, the edgy young men of Charlie Company, expecting a firefight and anxious to at last even the score for their comrades picked off by an invisible enemy, split into three platoons. Two were assigned to take up flank positions and block the escape of anyone from the village. The central platoon, consisting of some 30 men, commanded by Lieut. William Calley, 25, headed into the village. The Americans met no resistance on the outskirts. But despite the lack of enemy fire, Calley's men in less than 20 minutes ignited huts (or "hootches") and chased all the villagers—whether fleeing, standing or begging for mercy—into groups and shot every one of them. All were either elderly men, women or children. None—not one—was a Viet Cong male soldier. Estimates of the number of people slaughtered, even 40 years later, are not final;

the U.S. Army confirms that 347 died; the Vietnamese government estimate is around 500.

The stories soldiers later related of the massacre are brutal: let one account stand for all. At the court martial of Lieut. Calley in 1970, Dennis Conti, 21 in 1969 and a private first class in Calley's platoon, testified that after entering the village, he and fellow private Paul D. Meadlo held a group of 30 to 40 villagers—most of them women and children—on a path in My Lai at Calley's orders. When Calley returned, Conti testified, "He said, 'I thought I told you to take care of these people.' I said, 'We are. We're guarding them.' Calley said, 'No, kill them.' He said to come around to this side, get on line and fire into them. I told him I would guard a tree line, with my grenade launcher, while they fired.

"Calley and Meadlo got on line and fired directly into the people. They screamed and yelled. Some tried to get up. There were lots of heads and pieces of heads shot off, and flesh flew off the sides and arms and legs." Meadlo, Conti told the court, was now weeping. He tried to give his rifle to Conti. "I told him I couldn't," the witness

FIRES OF REVENGE *A U.S. soldier stokes the flames consuming a village hut; Americans called the homes "hootches"*

continued. "[I said] 'Let Lieut. Calley kill them' ... Some kids were still standing and Calley finished them off with single shots."

A second, larger group of civilians died in an irrigation ditch on the east side of My Lai. Conti approached, he said, and saw "Lieut. Calley and Sergeant [David] Mitchell standing on a dike, firing ... There were people in [the ditch] and Calley and Mitchell were firing into it ... I saw one woman try to get up. I saw Lieut. Calley fire and blow the side of her head off. So I left."

That is only one person's account of the slaughter; the court heard many more. Among the stories: one young American shot himself in the foot so he could escape the murder spree. He was the only U.S. casualty of the day's action.

FOR 18 LONG MONTHS, THE EVENTS AT MY LAI DID not come to light. The only people who reported the crimes at the time were the Viet Cong, who passed out leaflets publicizing the slaughter. To counter the V.C. accusation, regarded as standard propaganda, the U.S. Army launched a cursory field investigation, which "did not support" the charges. What put

My Lai on the front pages after 20 months was the conscience of Richard Ridenhour, 23, a former Specialist 4 who had known many of the men in Charlie Company and kept hearing about it. He was at first disbelieving, then deeply disturbed. In March 1969—a year after the slaughter—he sent copies of a letter with the information he had pieced together to the President, several Congressmen and some 30 other Washington officials.

Ridenhour's letter eventually led to a new probe—and to formal charges that were first brought to light by enterprising journalist Seymour Hersh, 32, reporting

All the victims were elderly men or women and children. None—not one—was a male Viet Cong soldier. One young American shot himself in the foot to escape taking part in the murder spree. He was the only U.S. casualty that day

for a little-known start-up news agency, the Dispatch News Service. On Sept. 5, 1969, just one day before he was to be released from the Army, charges of murdering "approximately 100" civilians at My Lai were preferred against Calley; 25 other officers and enlisted men were also initially charged.

In the months that followed, the full story of My Lai emerged in Army courts. On March 29, 1971, Calley was convicted of murder; two days later he was sentenced to life in prison. Within 48 hours, President Richard Nixon ordered him released—and the nation erupted in a fierce debate over whether justice had been served. In November 1974, Calley was officially paroled. No other U.S. soldiers were convicted in the massacre.

In the last week of 1971, in the final My Lai court martial, Brigade Commander Oran K. Henderson was acquitted of charges that he helped engineer the initial cover-up, which stated that the events at My Lai were a U.S. military victory in which 128 Viet Cong combatants had been killed, and some 20 civilians been inadvertently slain. "The first victim of war is truth," Rudyard Kipling once wrote. At My Lai, sadly, truth was all too quickly joined by other victims.

William Calley "A wonderful boy"

His hometown friends in Miami's northeast section called William Calley "Rusty," for his reddish-tinged brown hair. Mrs. Arnold Minkley, who lived across the street, remembered, "He was a wonderful boy, and would do anything for you." At Edison High School, Rusty was on the debate team, dated regularly, dressed well, drank beer with his buddies and kept things moving in any group. But he quit Palm Beach Junior College in Lake Worth after a year, dropping out with two Cs, one D and four Fs in his seven courses. "It just seemed like the 13th year in high school," Calley told TIME in 1970.

After he left college, he worked as a hotel bellhop, a restaurant dishwasher and a strikebreaking switchman on the Florida East Coast Railroad. In 1965, he started drifting west in a brand-new Buick Wildcat. He worked his way across the country to New Mexico, taking pictures of real estate for insurance appraisers from time to time. He enlisted in the U.S. Army in Albuquerque in mid-1966 and was soon recommended for officer candidate school, commissioned a lieutenant and posted to Vietnam.

After he was found guilty in a U.S. Army court martial in 1971 and was officially paroled three years later, Calley pursued a quiet life. Until recently he worked in a family jewelry store in a shopping mall in Columbus, Ga., but in the last few years he and his wife divorced and he moved to Atlanta, reportedly to live with his son. He turned 65 in 2009.

EYEWITNESSES *South Vietnamese civilians watch the murders; they may later have joined the ranks of those killed*

MARCHING FOR PEACE *Student protesters parade through the streets of Kent, Ohio, on Moratorium Day, Oct. 15, 1969. The young woman who*
Allison Krause, 19, who would be shot to death by members of the Ohio National Guard during protests at Kent State University in May 1970,

is shown clapping her hands above the word ALL *is student after President Richard Nixon ordered the invasion of Cambodia*

HOWARD RUFFNER

Bring the War Home!

A pair of mammoth protests reflects the nation's changing views of the war in Vietnam

AMERICANS WERE FOUR YEARS DEEP INTO THE nation's major intervention in Vietnam in 1969. As the war dragged on with little sign of winding down, sentiment against the U.S. commitment, once confined to small groups of students and activists, was shared by a broader spectrum of citizens. Frustrated with President Richard Nixon's slow progress in changing U.S. policy in Southeast Asia, national antiwar groups called for two major demonstrations in the fall of 1969: a nationwide Moratorium Day on Oct. 15, to be followed on Nov. 15 by a massive Mobilization of antiwar groups in the nation's capital. The first event proved to be the more striking of the two, as it reflected the widespread decrease in support for the war among Americans. The second event, in retrospect, seems to have been more an exercise in preaching to the choir: the Mobilization helped rally the spirits of antiwar groups, but unlike the Moratorium, it did not memorably reflect the changing national mood.

Moratorium Day, Oct. 15, 1969, was a landmark event in American history: one of the largest national protests against government policy ever held presented a series of wrenching contrasts. Across the country—in drenching San Francisco rain, in ankle-deep Denver snow, in crisp New York fall sunshine—Americans took part in a unique national observance. Quiet seminars mulled over the issues

Mobilizing *A huge crowd gathers at the Washington Monument on Nov. 15, 1969. Organizers of the Mobilization in the nation's capital declared that it attracted a larger crowd than the historic civil-rights march led by Martin Luther King Jr. in 1963*

of the war, while picketers shouted their dissent. Some mass marches developed a football rally spirit; elsewhere, a funereal atmosphere dominated as church bells tolled and the names of the war dead were read. One student at Houston's University of St. Thomas broke down and wept while reading a list of U.S. war dead; he had come to the name of a close friend whose death he was unaware of. In Indiana, four University of Notre Dame students burned their draft cards shortly before a "resistance Mass" was celebrated for some 2,500 on the library lawn.

"What was perhaps most striking," TIME noted, "was not the size of the hundreds of rallies and parades but rather the delicate balance temporarily achieved in many sections of the U.S. The formerly shattering voices of protest were more numerous than ever before, but at the same time less shrill. The old militant certainties of anti-communists have been tempered by the relentless persistence of the war."

In the White House, Richard Nixon spent much of the day reviewing Latin American policy, although his mind doubtless wandered occasionally to the events in his country. At Oxford University, Rhodes scholar Bill Clinton, 23, helped organize a vigil of protest, taking a stand that would later haunt him in his political career. In South Vietnam, an army platoon set out from Chu Lai on combat patrol and killed two guerrillas in a firefight. Half the members of the platoon wore the black armbands of Moratorium Day.

The day pointed up striking new rearrangements of politics and ideology—as when Lyndon Johnson's once intimate adviser, Bill Moyers, addressed a Wall Street crowd of 20,000, among them hundreds of bankers, on the mistaken war policies. At Minnesota's Macalester College, a grim Professor Hubert Humphrey heard his recent vice presidency and position on Vietnam roundly criticized by young fellow faculty members. In Massachusetts, a crowd of 100,000 filled the Boston Common. They were mostly students, but mothers from Newton and Wellesley walked among them. From a bar, a man hollered his opinion, "Bums! Do they think of the guys who died on Guadalcanal?"

In the Detroit suburb of Birmingham, a Republican enclave, more than 1,000 protested in Shain Park:

116

SOLIDARITY *In addition to the two major fall events, demonstrations were held throughout 1969 across the nation. On April 15 a large antiwar rally was held in New York City; above, protesters march up the Avenue of the Americas to Central Park*

18 TODAY, DEAD TOMORROW read one poster. "I fought hard in World War II," said a physician, James Pingel, "but I'm against this one. It's morally wrong. I've got two boys coming up." Malcolm Baldridge, co-chairman of the Connecticut Citizens for Nixon-Agnew in 1968, told a rally of 15,000 in New Haven, "The President should move faster to end the war."

THE ENORMOUS TURNOUTS AT IVY LEAGUE SCHOOLS were predictable reflections of their long histories of dissent. But the Moratorium also brought the antiwar movement to smaller, conservative colleges. Students at Kentucky's Jefferson Community College donated blood to the Red Cross as a constructive—and unorthodox—gesture of protest. At Richard Nixon's alma mater in California, Whittier College, 600 students attended a ceremony to light a "Flame of Life" set to burn until the war's end. Others at Whittier marched in support of Nixon.

Anti-Moratorium sentiment was strongest in the South and Midwest. Georgia Governor Lester Maddox railed against "longhairs, hippies, socialists and communists" and led a chorus of *God Bless America* on the capitol steps. Red, white and blue arm bands sprouted in such cities as Beaumont, Texas, where the city council declared a "Support Our Boys in Vietnam Day."

The mood was different one month later, when the Mobilization effort brought some 250,000 protesters to the nation's capital on a bitterly cold day. Near the Washington Monument, folksinger Pete Seeger led the huge crowd in singing *Give Peace a Chance*. But if the day turned ugly, as it did when some 6,000 protesters were tear-gassed in clashes with police in front of the Justice Department, the event made its point: opposition to the war was not confined to "an effete corps of impudent snobs," as Vice President Spiro Agnew had so memorably declared. The protesters from every state, from all age groups and stations of life who paraded through the capital embodied a broad-based antiwar movement that had become a potent force—so potent that its influence must be taken into account by the Administration. By marching in the streets, the antiwar voices had earned a place, however begrudged, at the tables of deliberation.

Rock 'n' Reality

At a California festival, music's age of innocence ends in death

WELL, IT WAS FUN WHILE IT LASTED. THE AGE OF Aquarius ended with the flash of a knife on Dec. 6, 1969, at a tumble-down raceway near Altamont Pass, Calif., outside San Francisco. The Hell's Angels motorcycle club had been engaged to guard the stage at a free concert given by the Rolling Stones to celebrate the end of their highly successful American tour. Joining the Stones on the bill were some of the best American West Coast bands, including the Jefferson Airplane and the Grateful Dead. It was the Dead who suggested that their bad-ass biker buddies, the Hell's Angels, could serve, informally, as security.

Bad idea. The Angels had never had a problem in shepherding the Dead's mellow fans at small outdoor concerts—but by the time some 300,000 people gathered at the racetrack, there were bad vibrations all around. The venue was a last-minute choice, and there were no preparations to handle the huge crowd. The audience was tense and anxious, and the Angels, armed with weighted pool cues and other implements of destruction, were all too willing to fight. Several minor skirmishes broke out during the afternoon, and after Marty Balin of the Jefferson Airplane was decked by an Angel when he attempted to intervene in a struggle right in front of the stage, the Dead refused to perform.

By the time the Stones appeared, several heads had been busted and the fans were in a frightened, surly mood. Even Mick Jagger, then rock's definitive superstar, could not get them to cool down and listen to the music. The crowd pushed closer and closer to the stage, and the Angels angrily pushed them back. Suddenly a fan, Meredith Hunter, 18, pulled a gun. The Angels went after him, knifed him down and did him in. Those close enough to the incident were appalled. Those who were not quickly caught the mood of tragedy and left the concert silent and shaken. (Angel Alan Passaro was tried for murder but was acquitted in 1972 on grounds of self-defense.) It was hard to believe that Woodstock had taken place just four months before. Dying with a whimper, the '60s were history.

SYMPATHY FOR THE DEVIL? *Not this time. A caped Jagger and the*

band stopped playing at one point, above, then continued. Their paeans to primal urges morphed from metaphor into murder at Altamont

THE VETERAN *At home in Barnstable in 1969, age 46. With* Slaughterhouse-Five, *Vonnegut achieved the goal he told* TIME *in 1969 that he sought: to escape the "literary ghetto" of being regarded as a science-fiction writer rather than a mainstream novelist*

Kurt Vonnegut Jr.

With *Slaughterhouse-Five,* he peers through the glass of the past, darkly

O N A WALL IN THE STUDY OF HIS TWO-STORY home in Barnstable, Mass., in 1969, writer Kurt Vonnegut hung a sign bearing this message: GOD DAMN IT YOU GOT TO BE KIND. That command, TIME declared on reviewing his 1969 novel, *Slaughterhouse-Five,* was the core message of Vonnegut's work, however obscured by sci-fi fantasies, absurdist philosophizing and shockingly bleak humor. "For all his roundhouse swinging at punch-card culture," TIME noted, "his satiric forays are really an appeal for a return to Christ-like behavior in a world never conspicuously able to follow Christ's example. For Vonnegut, man's worst folly is a persistent attempt to adjust, smoothly, rationally, to the unthinkable, to the unbearable. Misused, modern science is its prime instrument."

In *Slaughterhouse-Five,* today widely considered his masterpiece, Vonnegut confronted head-on the demons that haunted him: his experience as a prisoner of war who survived the Allied fire-bombing of Dresden in World War II, which left a great city in ruins and tens of thousands of civilians dead. In the novel, Vonnegut's stand-in, Billy Pilgrim, witnesses the bombing of Dresden, then becomes "unstuck in time" and is captured by aliens—all the better to gain perspective on the folly and cruelty of man. The novel's pessimistic, gloomy refrain—"So it goes"— expresses the angst that would lead its author to a failed suicide attempt in 1984.

"Vonnegut could easily have become a crank," TIME's Lev Grossman wrote after his death in 2007, "but he was too smart; he could have become a cynic, but there was something tender in his nature that he could never quite suppress; he could have become a bore, but even at his most despairing he had an endless willingness to entertain his readers—with drawings, jokes, sex, bizarre plot twists, science fiction, whatever it took." More rueful than defeated, he struggled to be kind.

Philip Roth
A major novelist extends a hand—but would you shake it?

THERE'S NO NEED FOR A SECOND OPINION AS TO the complaint that afflicts Alexander Portnoy, the decidedly unheroic narrator and namesake of Philip Roth's hilarious 1969 novel, because you'll never top Portnoy's own diagnosis. As he explains, he is "torn by desires that are repugnant to my conscience, and a conscience repugnant to my desires." To no one's surprise, when Roth unleashed the story of his conflicted Jewish Everyman upon mainstream America early in 1969, it was the repugnance of those desires rather than the calls of his conscience that set tongues awagging and sales asoaring. As TIME explained, "In the most explicit detail ever bound between the covers of a best seller, Portnoy relives his adolescent masturbations … the more he discharged, the greater became his guilt. It was a vicious cycle that led him into his psychological ghetto of lust and shame."

On further examination, it turned out that Portnoy inhabited a wide and revealing variety of ghettos: as a modern-day Jew reared by a domineering mother and an emasculated father; as a product of 20th century American consumer culture; as a male in the late 1960s, exploring the sexual revolution from the front lines.

Yet as he had demonstrated in such earlier works as the novella *Goodbye, Columbus*, Roth, 36 in 1969, was both an acerbic critic of U.S. culture and a born entertainer, and in *Portnoy's Complaint* he created a rarity in fiction: a comic masterpiece at novel length. Stretched out on the couch of his psychoanalyst, Dr. Spielvogel, Portnoy became America's first lie-down comic, embodying not only the tics of a man trying to disentangle himself from his background but also the latent fear of the liberal humanist that he may find himself out. Happily for Portnoy's gifted creator, *Goodbye, Columbus*, was brought to the screen in fine form in 1969—making it a breakthrough year for a novelist who has continued to probe the American scene with gusto, raunch and redeeming insights.

DICKENS OF THE DELI *Revisiting old haunts, Roth saunters through the streets of Newark, N.J., his boyhood home, in 1969*